How to Listen to a Sermon

With "Honoring the Gospel" and Other Homilies for the Sake of Heaven

Donald L. Berry

UNIVERSITY PRESS OF AMERICA,® INC.
Lanham • Boulder • New York • Toronto • Plymouth, UK

Copyright © 2011 by
University Press of America,® Inc.
4501 Forbes Boulevard
Suite 200
Lanham, Maryland 20706
UPA Acquisitions Department (301) 459-3366

Estover Road
Plymouth PL6 7PY
United Kingdom

All rights reserved
Printed in the United States of America
British Library Cataloging in Publication Information Available

Library of Congress Control Number: 2010931768
ISBN: 978-0-7618-5315-2 (paperback : alk. paper)
eISBN: 978-0-7618-5316-9

∞ ™ The paper used in this publication meets the minimum
requirements of American National Standard for Information
Sciences—Permanence of Paper for Printed Library Materials,
ANSI/NISO Z39.48-1992.

In Grateful Memory
of
Warren Clement Ramshaw
[1926–2005]

Fond Faithful Friend

Contents

Preface	vii

PART I CRAFT AND HOMILY

1 Poetics of Homily	3
2 How to Listen to a Sermon	9
3 Honoring the Gospel	12

PART II HOMILIES FOR THE SAKE OF HEAVEN

4 In Ordinary Time	19
Hebrews 12:1, "Run"	19
Mark 14:45, "Ransom"	22
John 6:24-35, "I Am the Bread of Life"	25
Collect for Proper 28, "The Sun of Righteousness"	29
Collect for Proper 28, "Inwardly Digesting Holy Scripture"	32
Psalm 34:8, "Tasting God"	35
John 6:52-58, "Companions and Critics of Christ"	39
Romans 5:1-17, "A Bible-Centered Church?"	42
Mark 10:2-16, "The Right Thing to Do"	46
Mark 9:30-37, "Being First and Last"	48
Ephesians 6:10-20, "Put on the Whole Armor of God"	51
II Corinthians 12:2-10, "My Grace Is Sufficient for Thee"	55
John 15:9-17, "On Being Commanded to Love"	58
Mark 4:41, "They Feared a Great Fear"	60
Matthew 25:15-22, "Give to Caesar . . ."	63
Mark 8:27-38, Questions the Bible Asks	66

5 In Extraordinary Times	71
Advent, Luke 21:25-36, "The Intrusion of Grace"	71
Advent, Matthew 24:36-44, "The Distant Scene"	74
Advent, Philippians 4:4-7, "Nevertheless, Rejoice"	77
Christmas, Luke 2:1-20 KJV, "The Ponder Heart"	79
Epiphany, Matthew 2:1-12, "With the Lens of the Incarnation"	82
Epiphany, John 1:29-42, "Where Are You Staying, Jesus?"	85
Transfiguration, Matthew 17:1-19, "Transfigurations"	87
Lent, John 3:1-17, "The Writing on the Wall"	90
Lent, John 9:1-27, "Faith as a Way of Seeing"	93
Easter Day, John 20:10-18, "The Resurrection as God's Endorsement"	96
Eastertide, John 10:1-10, "More Life than Before"	99
Eastertide, John 14:1-6, "Let Not Your Heart Be Troubled"	102
Ascension Day, Acts 1:1-11, "Why Do You Stand Looking Up toward Heaven?"	104
Pentecost, I Corinthians 12:7, "The Lord, the Giver of Life"	107
6 Living an Epiphany	110
Other Books by Donald L. Berry	115

Preface

During the intermission in a Sunday afternoon concert by the Colgate University Orchestra, I was chatting on the Chapel steps with one of my faculty colleagues. He knew, of course, that in addition to a full-time University teaching program, I also had been for many years a very part-time rector of a small Episcopal parish a half-hour drive from Hamilton, with primarily Sunday morning obligations, and that on occasion I still officiated on Sunday morning in other parishes in the Diocese of Central New York. And so it was perfectly natural for him to ask, quite cordially, "Did you preach someplace this morning?"

He could not have put the question in a simpler and more straightforward manner. Yet I found myself uncertain how to respond, for I placed as much value as did he on needing to be as clear as possible about saying what we mean when we speak. We had both taught Plato's *Phaedo* in Colgate's General Education program, and knew well Socrates' admonition: "To express oneself badly is not only faulty as far as the language goes, but does some harm to the soul. . . . There is no greater evil one can suffer than to hate reasonable discourse."[1]

After what must have seemed a peculiarly long pause, I acknowledged that I was not quite sure just how to respond to what I called his very Protestant question, but that the short answer was "Yes." But I also knew that this short answer was misleading. "I did give a sermon this morning," I said, "but 'preaching a sermon' is not a very clear act description of what happened . . ." "Well," he replied, "if you spoke in church but didn't 'preach a sermon' just what did you do?"

That question, I realized, traded on his memories of more than three decades earlier when I was a University Chaplain, Protestant then by membership if not sensibility, and "delivered sermons" regularly in the Colgate Memorial Chapel, sometimes but rarely, in my colleague's hearing. He more likely had read some of them, however, since these sermonic essays were frequently published for wider campus distribution, and he could have had easy access to their argument without their liturgical frame – albeit a rather spare one in that very Puritan setting.

So I continued, "I did 'do a sermon' this morning, but not at all the sort of thing I used to do as a chaplain." There was another long pause, occasioned this time by the dawning realization that I had not yet raised to a level of full self-consciousness the way the sermon project had developed for me in more recent years, and since that Chapel step conversation had evolved even more. The conceptuality that did occur to me, I thought, would very likely be puzzling to my colleague, who was concerned that formal utterance be discursive and clear. "The nearest model I can suggest at the moment, the one that comes closes to what I think of myself as doing when it comes time for the sermon, is "'poetry reading,' perhaps 'poetry reading with commentary.'"

In "The Poetics of Homily" I will explain what was in my mind on that occasion, and will advance some suggestions about the way a sermon might so function as to meet what I regard as its defining qualities.[2] The sermon must be intellectually honest, liturgically appropriate, faithful to the liberating insights and life-enhancing power of the Christian Gospel, and sensitive to the life-situation and the inviolable conscience of the listener. These four conditions seem to me to be those features which anyone preaching ought to hold himself or herself responsible for trying to meet.

Those who preach regularly seldom have opportunities to hear others preach. But I have found one or another of these requirements often violated by much of the preaching that I have heard. The most frequent and seriously destructive homiletical fault that I have observed has been the failure to be intellectually honest, that is, the unwillingness or the inability to incorporate, in appropriate ways, the best available scholarship in commenting on the biblical texts. Such a failure conveys to a congregation a false view of biblical literature, and of the peculiar sort of authority it can have for the religious life. It almost always fails to respect the genre of the writing it seeks to elucidate. That is especially significant, since recognizing the genre of a text is crucial for its understanding. A poem means differently from the way a letter, a folk tale, a genealogy, a prophetic oracle, or an event description means.

The homiletical perspective that I outline and hope to illustrate here aims to meet the concerns of these desiderata, but it is not intended to be judgmental or prescriptive. It is offered, rather, as a suggestion, a reflection on my own developing experiences in the pulpit. This approach is my attempt to think about the sermon and the preaching event in a different way, and perhaps to think through the peculiar power and possibility that attach to the sermonic occasion when attention is paid to its appeal to the religious imagination.[3]

Although this perspective was nurtured and is most naturally at home in the sacramental worship of the Anglican tradition, the homiletical action in the churches of other, non-catholic traditions also might be renovated by taking this position into account.

The sermon in this context may very well elucidate some biblical or theological issue, convey some ethical recommendations, or clarify the relevance of the Gospel of Incarnate Love to some contemporary dilemma, but its primary purpose and defining character cannot be exclusively identified with any of these important goals. The perspective outlined here assumes and requires that venues be found for theological and biblical instruction, moral exhortation, and the discussion of contemporary issues other than the regular parish celebration of the Holy Eucharist. Engaging in such tasks, clearly necessary for the on-going life and work of Christian communities, cannot occupy the sermon in a central way without doing violence to the imaginal and illuminative character of the homiletical moment.

I want to express my gratitude to St. James' Church in Goshen, Indiana, where I first sensed the religious power and truth of the Anglo-Catholic vision, long before it was so explicitly acknowledged in the *Book of Common Prayer*, that the Holy Eucharist is "the principal act of Christian worship on the Lord's Day and other major Feasts." [p. 13]

I am happy also to acknowledge the appreciative comment and generous response of many persons in those ten parishes of the Diocese of Central York, where I have preached and celebrated for extended periods: St. Thomas' [Hamilton], where I was ordained to the Sacred Order of Priests; St. George's [Chadwicks], St. Stephen's [New Hartford], St. Mark's [Chenango Bridge], Grace [Baldwinsville], St. James' [Clinton], Grace [Utica], , Grace [Mexico], St. Paul's [Chittenango], and Epiphany [Sherburne]. Worshipping with them has confirmed for me the very close relationship of sermon and sacrament. Both sermon and sacrament aim for the transformation of life; their difference is a formal one, for both have power by virtue of a respect for the religious imagination. To hold the chalice as central is to recognize that what is most important cannot be spoken, but must be acted. Nonetheless, what one does speak matters in very important ways. The essay and examples that follow are an attempt to suggest how that takes place.

A friendly witness to the serious craft of sermon preparation and preaching is "On Listening to a Sermon," the source of the title of this book, which I am happy and grateful to acknowledge: "How to Listen to a Sermon." This is a revised, edited, amplified, and in some parts rewritten version of an essay whose original voice was that of Warren C. Ramshaw [1926-2005],[4] one of the most theologically literate and informed lay persons of the Episcopal Church in recent years. It was a teaching unit in his 1999 Confirmation Class at St. Thomas' Church, Hamilton, NY. I was serving in an interim capacity at St. Thomas' during this period, and my homiletical craft and preaching style are clearly presupposed in his suggestions about how to listen to a sermon.[5] It should not be difficult to apply his advice about "listening" to a sermon to "reading" a sermon. Readers are invited to consider how his comments might illuminate their own sermon preparation and/or their own sermon listening and reading.

"Listening," of course, does not exhaust the ways in which one might respond to a sermon. "Listening" is the project for a worshipper who seeks to "understand," to be newly motivated. But there are other less intellectual homiletical outcomes that are sometimes appropriate, or not predictable: joining an appeal, enlisting in a cause, sighing with a heart newly warmed.

Preaching in our churches would likely be improved were a priest supported by a congregation of which a significant number had the education and homiletical expectations presupposed by "How to Listen to a Sermon." But such an experience would be a daunting one, indeed!

NOTES

1. Plato, *Phaedo*,115e, 89c,d.
2. I have explored some of this in my "Thinking about Preaching," in *Holy Words and Holy Orders* [Lanham, MD., University Press of America, 2009], pp. 20-21.
3. The concern to re-envision the sermon that takes into fuller account matters of the religious imagination is not, of course, unique to me. In his article, "The Book of *Job* and the *Tae Te Ching* as Antidotes to 'Preachy' Preaching" [*Anglican Theological Review,* Vol. LXXIV, No. 3, Summer 1992, pp. 370-378], David J. Schlafer has reflected on how attention to Stephen Mitchell's recent translation of *The Book of Job* [San Francisco: North Point Press, 1986], and *Tao Te Chin g* [New York: Harper and Row, 1988], might encourage the preacher to avoid heavy-handed didactic preaching by becoming open to a non-persuasive, more indirect homiletical technique. Although he does not construct a homiletical model as such, Schlafer at least begins to suggest how a non-persuasive approach might allow the sermon to make "space for the Spirit." One needs always to leave "space for worshippers to sense and respond to the Word itself." [p. 34] The perspective of the present essay resonates with this interest.
4. Warren C. Ramshaw [1926-2005] was an active participant in the life of the Episcopal Church on the national, diocesan, and parish levels for many years. At St. Thomas' Church in Hamilton, NY, he had been warden, vestry member, treasurer, lector, Eucharistic Minister, teacher. In the Diocese of Central New York he had been a member of the Standing Committee, Commission on Ministry, member of the Search Committee for the Tenth Bishop, and eight times a Deputy to General

Convention. Member of the Executive Committee for Province II. For the National Church, he had been Chair of the Board for Theological Education, Chair of the General Board of Examining Chaplains, member of the Council of Advice to the President of the House of Deputies, and a member of the Whitaker Committee on Human Sexuality.

5. Ramshaw's guide to listening trades on such considerations of a carefully crafted sermon as these: opening and closing lines, central images, repetition, variation, contrast, word-play, etc. A priest who saw Ramshaw's teaching instruction thought it did not sufficiently take into account the freedom of the Holy Spirit to seize the homiletical moment, so to speak. Ramshaw's response to this alleged danger was to suggest that openness to the sudden work of the Holy Spirit is not opposed to or thwarted by careful thought, and should not be seen as a way to avoid the hard work of thoughtful reflection and writing. These acts are guided by the Holy Spirit as well.

Part I

CRAFT AND HOMILY

Chapter One

Poetics of Homily

In the Preface I related a conversation I once had with a colleague that turned on an understanding of the distinctive character of the sermon or homily.[1] Clarifying the identity of the sermon requires us to distinguish between the sermon as an answer to the "Protestant question," and the sermon as a peculiar speech act in the context of Anglican reflection and praise.

In the Anglican tradition, the homily is the verbal, interpretive act that intends, in the context of the celebration of the Holy Eucharist as framed in the *Book of Common Prayer*, to enable the biblical lections that it follows [from which it takes its cue, and whose servant it is] to become revelatory of the divine intention and possibility for human life. A sermon aims to do in a literary and spoken way what the Holy Eucharist does in an enacted narrative manner—to re-present, that is to make present again, the nurturing, liberating and empowering work of God as this is disclosed in the career of Jesus of Nazareth, whom faith perceives as the human face and embodiment of the fullness of God.

What the sermon or homily ought to be and do is not self-evident, especially when one takes into consideration the liturgical and sacramental context in which it regularly and most appropriately occurs, at least for the tradition defined and served by the *Book of Common Prayer*.

For some, the sermon is thought to appeal primarily to the mind or the intellect, with the basic intention to explain some theological or biblical enigma, claim, or counsel. For others, the sermonic discourse appeals primarily to the will, having its basic intention to exhort the hearer to act, or to refrain from acting, in a specified way. Others view the homiletic occasion as an opportunity to address a contemporary issue in the light of relevant biblical insight, appealing thus to both the will and the intellect.

For still others the sermon is a charismatic event for which neither the intellect nor the will is central. Here the appeal is to the emotions, and the preacher's goal is to enable the listeners to feel a particular way.

Without intending to demean the occasional usefulness of these approaches, the position suggested here views the homily as appealing in a special way to the imagination. This is what I had in mind when I volunteered "poetry reading" as an account of what I had done when I "delivered a sermon" that morning.

This understanding of the homily as an imaginal event draws on an important distinction between the substance and perspective of the Christian reality. Every ecclesial expression of Christian faith receives its distinctive character by virtue of the way in which the relationship between these two defining factors is perceived and nourished. Accordingly, the service will be kept from being simply a "preaching" event by the preacher's recognition and awareness that the sermon is neither an insular nor an exhaustive speech acct, but a vocal event that is always in relation to the substantive and perspectival dimensions of Christian faith.

Of the several ways in which these community-shaping elements have been identified, four conceptual strategies have been most widely employed. Recalling the elements in any one of these four configurations can prevent us from thinking of the sermon alone as the defining event when the parish gathers to praise.

[1] Paul Tillich termed the Christian polarities "the catholic substance" and "the protestant principle."[2] He was concerned to make clear that this typology does not refer in a simple, univocal way, to the Roman Catholic Church and to the churches of the Protestant Reformation respectively. Rather, "catholic substance" names the visible features of the tradition, such as ritual acts, doctrinal formulations and creedal statements, authoritative texts, and offices of interpretation, leadership, and administration.

The Chicago-Lambeth Quadrilateral [1886, 1888] that accounts the following as ingredients essential to the restoration of ecclesiastical union, can be regarded as one attempt to specify the content of the "catholic substance": the Bible, the creeds of the undivided church [Apostles' and Nicene], the dominical sacraments [Baptism and the Holy Eucharist], and the historic episcopate.

In this view the "protestant principle" is the cautionary voice speaking against idolatry, a "prophetic" perspective that alerts the churches to their constant need to avoid investing any of the finite forms of ecclesial life with absolute value or infallible status.

Properly employed the "protestant principle," as such, relativizes all human goods and achievements, particularly, in this case, Scripture, creeds, ritual acts, authoritative offices, and patterns of ecclesial organization. In the light of the "protestant principle," no aspect of the "catholic substance" can be regarded as an end in itself, since all church forms, even the most hallowed and venerable, are means—imperfect and historically conditioned—to the end of transforming human life.

But in the light of the weight of the "catholic substance," no homiletical act can be regarded simply as a discrete, standing-alone, speech event.

[2] A second way of conceptualizing the polarities of the Christian life is to speak of the "sacramental" and the "prophetic." This terminology has an advantage over Tillich's typology in that it lessens the possibility of being easily identified with the empirical realities of Roman Catholic and Protestant churches, and seems, at first glance, to accord with the two parts of the mass-the proclamatory or instructional, and the Eucharist itself.

This terminology, however, is problematic in other ways. It trades on the special biblical sense of the prophetic—a warning against the idolatrous tendency of human life. But in most contemporary speech situations, "prophetic" always needs to be explained, since "prophetic" has come to mean "predictive" rather than "critical", and it is only the latter posture that is an expression of the "protestant principle."

Further, the term "sacramental" for many Christians seems to beg the question. Although Baptism and the Eucharist—in varying forms and procedures—are practiced in all Christian groups [save the Society of Friends], many Protestant companies regard these ritual acts as "ordinances" rather than "sacraments," understand them as memorial rather than sacrifice, attach no salvific value to their performance, and do not regard them as conferring grace, that is, as sacramental in any significant way.

When the "sacramental" and the "prophetic" are so understood, the homily will serve primarily a proclamatory purpose. Its intent will be so to announce the demand for justice that human relationships might more consistently conform to the divine mandate to respect the dignity of every person.

But when the "prophetic" is seen always in relation to the "sacramental," the sermon will not be regarded simply as the voice of the preacher, but the voice of the lively tradition in which he or she stands.

[3] A third way of naming these community-shaping categories has been suggested by F. W. Dillistone, who speaks of the "organic" and the "covenantal."[3] This manner of speaking has the advantage of taking seriously the "body" metaphor so prominent in the biblical characterization of the Christian community, and appreciating the reality of development which has always been regarded more positively by the catholic communities [Roman,

Anglican, Orthodox] than by the Protestant churches [both magisterial and free church].[4]

Viewing ecclesial life as organic enables one to give due importance and value to those forms [creed, sacrament, office, etc.] that are believed to represent the saving event of Jesus as the Christ. Such forms are, on analogy, as life-giving and life-expressing as those limbs and organs that give human existence its characteristic structure as it develops during its historical life.

On the other hand, the idea of covenant may not be so adequate a way to term the contrasting pole. It is, to be sure, closely related to the prophetic or protestant principle. As such, it is the model for the critical stance of the ancient Hebrew prophets who considered the life situation of Israel—especially the activities of its kings, priests, merchants—in violation of the normative requirements of the covenant, the life to which the people liberated from Egyptian servitude, and their descendants, are called.

Nonetheless, Dillistone himself recognizes that while the idea of covenant seems especially characteristic of the Reformed tradition, with its emphasis on divine election, the Lutheran emphasis on forgiveness and the loving community is not easily brought under the purview of the covenant idea.[5]

When the organic and covenantal are so understood, the homily will serve a proclamatory purpose, but related always to the inherited body of faith, belief, and practice. In this way the homily will aim to nourish the order, life, and work of the parish as a faith community.

[4] The fourth conceptual strategy does not point initially to empirical features of the Christian tradition as such, but seeks to identify contrasting perspectives or sensibilities, the differing dynamics that seem to be at work in ecclesial life. David Tracy has proposed a terminology that can help us understand the various forms and functions that the homily has come to have in the several Christian communions, and to see how the homily in the Anglican tradition can most appropriately be regarded as an imaginal event.[6] Tracy identifies the dynamic in Christian perception and expression, and the variety of ways in which the tension between Word and Sacrament is experienced as the function of two types of imagination: the analogical and the dialectical.[7]

Analogy and dialectic are two ways in which theology has historically attempted to interpret the substance of the Christian revelation in an always contemporary context. The analogical imagination employs "a rain forest of metaphors,"[8] seeks for signs of God's presence in the world, says that "God is like . . . ," appreciates myriad manifestations of the divine in the created order, and enjoys the devotions and liturgical practices that express and facilitate growth in grace. The dialectic imagination is the great "yes—but—no," acknowledges God's absence, hiddenness, and radical unlikeness.

The analogical and the dialectical thus clarify the content and style of different ecclesial constellations, and although these two ways might seem more explanatory of Catholic and Protestant phenomena, respectively, they are not mutually exclusive.[9] Neither is completely or only present in any religious community, and both are necessary if the evangelical virtues of Christian faith are to be experienced in their fullness, and if the homily is to be free to do its empowering work.

The priest is not called to be a poet, but a preacher who recognizes the rhetorical peculiarity of the sermon. At some level, and in the sacred secrecy of priestly reflection, the preacher needs to consider from time to time the way in which the sermon appeals to and depends on the imagination, not the intellect or the emotions alone. This can help to assure that we are indeed "fed in these holy mysteries," by God's graceful action at both the pulpit and the holy table.

NOTES

1. I use "homily" and "sermon" interchangeably. It seems to me that the same basic requirements hold without respect to length or formality.

2. Paul Tillich, *Systematic Theology* [Chicago: The University of Chicago Press, 1963], Vol. III, p. 6.

3. F. W. Dillistone, *The Structure of the Divine Society* [London: Lutterworth Press, 1951], p. 6.

4. Some Protestant groups regard all that happened between the second and sixteenth centuries as religiously disastrous.

5. Dillistone, pp. 248-255.

6. David Tracy, *The Analogical Imagination* [New York: Crossroad Books, 1981].

7. This distinction between the two modes of the religious imagination resonates with Tillich's distinction between two types of the philosophy of religion. With its emphasis on divine immanence, the ontological approach [Augustine] is similar to the analogical. With its emphasis on divine transcendence, the cosmological approach [Aquinas] is closer to the dialectical. According to Tillich, everything depends on the relationship between these two types. For him the ontological is foundational, and the use of the cosmological is dependent upon it. Without that kind of relationship the conflict between religion and culture cannot be reconciled. [Paul Tillich, "The Two Types of Philosophy of Religion," Theology of Culture, ed. Robert C. Kimball {New York: Oxford University Press, 1959}, pp. 10-29.

8. Source of this phrase is lost.

9. Andrew Greeley has employed Tracy's model of the analogical and dialectical imaginations as a way of understanding the various kinds of religious sensibility. Although he does not find either mode wholly or exclusively present in any one religious denomination, he regularly refers to the analogical as the "Catholic" imagina-

tion, and the dialectical as the "Protestant" imagination. This manner of speaking has the same difficulty as we observed earlier in Tillich's use of "catholic substance" and "protestant principle." The analysis of neither Greeley nor Tillich adequately deals with the catholic dimension of the Anglican tradition. See Andrew Greeley, "Protestant and Catholic: Is the Analogical Imagination Extinct?" *American Sociological Review*, Vol. 54, 19889, pp. 485-502; also Theology and Society: On Validating David Tracy," *Journal of the American Academy of Religion*, Vol. LIX, No. 4, Winter 1991, pp. 643-652.

Chapter Two

How to Listen to a Sermon[1]

Listening to a sermon is different from listening to other forms of public address. Clues to the message of a sermon are found not only in the text of the sermon but in the surrounding material—hymns, psalms, collects, prayers—that make up the service, of which the sermon is one part. Unlike many other forms of public speech, sermons are relatively short, probably about ten to twelve minutes, or fifteen at the most. Thus, the preacher must make the point to be conveyed, or the picture to be clarified, rather soon in the message, and establish the sermon's argument clearly and with emphasis. Opening material may set up a contrast with the major point the preacher wants to make. The contrast will usually make the essence of the argument stand out by relief. Usually, the sermon makes one central point, rather than a number of points.

Realize that as "audience" to a sermon, you are expected to work with the preacher to grasp the sermon's central message. This is often hard work, and it requires serious attention. A sermon is not entertainment, but an attempt to teach or to illuminate or explain a point out of the Lessons from the lectionary, to lift up an image or picture for reflection, or perhaps to inform the congregation about a matter of church history or biblical understanding related to the Lessons appointed for the day.

Here are some suggestions to help you prepare for and "listen" seriously to a sermon:

1. The Lessons appointed for each Sunday are the usual sources for the sermon's ideas. Therefore, reading the Lessons appointed for the day is the best way to recognize the themes the preacher may have selected for his or her preaching text. You can always find the Collect and the Lessons for any day identified in the Prayer Book They are also regularly announced a week ahead in the Sunday worship bulletin. Read these before coming

to Church, or come early enough to read them in the bulletin before the service.
2. Can you identify some themes or threads that tie these various Lessons and Prayers together? Those who created the Lectionary assume there is some kind of link between these elements.[2]
3. As the service unfolds, look especially at the words of the hymns [brief poetic windows into the Church's theology]. Do their words pick up or emphasize any of the themes in the Lessons?
4. When the sermon begins, listen closely to the first sentence or two. The "bait" for the ideas to be emphasized in the sermon is often hinted at here. Remember the first ideas may be the ones that are set up as a contrast with the major ideas the preacher wants to emphasize.
5. Can you make a simple outline of the points or the steps if the argument the sermon makes, or the pictures, phrases or images that will be the focus of the sermon? Imagine the preacher is speaking *only* to you. Focus your attention on the preacher's face, not just the preacher's gestures or motions. This may help you identify sentences or ideas the preacher feels strongly about. These may be clues to what the preacher wants to stress.
6. What words or terms are used more frequently than others? If you do not understand the meaning of a word or term, try writing it down, spelling it the best you can, so that you can look it up later, or ask someone what the word you did not understand actually is. It is quite alright later to ask the preacher about a word that you did not understand.
7. Listen closely to the way the sermon ends, to the last one or two sentences. If you have been listening carefully, you may be able to recognize when the sermon is drawing to a close. The overall point will undoubtedly be stated here. Even if you are not confident that you got *the* point of the sermon, jot down the point or points you understood. They may become clear to you later.
8. Later, after the service, but while the experience of the sermon is still fresh in your mind, write down in one or two sentences what you understood the major message of the sermon to have been. Imagine that you want to tell a friend about the sermon in just a few words. What would you say? Write down your words. A day or two later read you notes again, and see if something further comes to mind. You could even go back to read the Collect and the Lessons from the service leaflet [remember to carry one home], or look them up again in your Bible. The Prayer Book lectionary will remind you what the Lessons were that were appointed for that service. Doing this may remind you of some of the insights the sermon presented.

9. Don't give up. Listening, like seeing or reading or speaking, is a skill that takes practice. It will not happen in one attempt. If your parents heard the sermon, talk over the ideas as you understood them with them. Do your conclusions agree with those of your parents? Where do they differ? Sometimes copies of the sermon are made available to interested members of the congregation. Should you have access in this way to the text of a sermon you have heard, check to see if what you have read confirms what you have listened to.

Next time come to class with some ideas or questions to share with others to see, collectively, what we have learned from the sermon. Bring your notes with you.

NOTES

1. As noted in the Preface [end note #4], the origin of this chapter was a confirmation class exercise designed by Warren C. Ramshaw, October 3, 1999, for St. Thomas' Church, Hamilton, NY.

2. This assumption informs the Lectionary in the *Book of Common Prayer*. Track One, however, of the *Revised Common Lectionary* is based on different principles, so that connections among the Lessons may not be evident, or present at all. Track Two of the RCL is closer to the Prayer Book Lectionary.

Chapter Three

Honoring the Gospel

1

Reading the Gospel from the pulpit is neither my personal preference, nor a liturgical action that clearly recognizes the high value that the Gospel texts have for Christian faith and life.

I prefer to read the Gospel down the aisle among the congregation, with the Gospel Book held by an acolyte, preceded by the Crucifer, flanked by candle-bearers, and, if not every time, at least on special occasions such as Christmas Eve, Easter Day, and Pentecost and All Saints, perhaps accompanied by incense.

But I am unlikely to do that very often any more. Although reading the Gospel right here, from the pulpit, may not best symbolize the importance of these holy texts, it does have some liturgical and theological justification.

Consider this: Having the Gospel read from the pulpit where the sermon is to be preached immediately afterwards should remind the preacher quite dramatically that the sermon is not an occasion to express his or her personal opinions on some topic.

In some way or other, the sermon must always speak the Gospel word of forgiveness, the Gospel word of justice-making, the Gospel call to Church-upbuilding. The sermon must attend, in some way, to some word, some image, to some promise, or some admonition in the Lessons that have just been read, and especially to the Gospel's promise of new life.

The preacher must always assume that there will be someone in the congregation this very day who seriously needs to hear, to be reminded, to be told afresh that God will wipe the slate clean, that God gives so graciously what we need deep down, but could never achieve on our own. I believe this to be true, and believe that it is a sufficient liturgical and theological justification for having the Gospel read precisely where the sermon is to be preached.

For it is the Gospel truth, not the preacher's personal project or anxiety that must be given voice. The preacher must always allow that someone will be present and listening that very day who seriously needs to hear God's offer of salvation, whether it is phrased in an interesting way or not.

I believe this to be true, and it surely justifies having the Gospel read precisely where the sermon is to be preached. Yet my preference and the best liturgical advice are all otherwise.

As appropriate as reading from the pulpit may be, my reason for reading the Gospel here rather than down in the aisle among the people, is quite different, and much simpler, and quite without theological overtones.

I do not read from this spot to make a theological or liturgical point, but simply because I am much more physically comfortable reading where I have a piece of furniture nearby for support.

I am basically mobile, but I do not walk much distance with ease, and I realize that sometimes I tend to weave a bit if I stand, unaided, very long. For some time I have aimed to do only minimal walking in the service. Not to make a liturgical statement, but simply to avoid teetering a little, and not to lose my balance.

An old Gospel hymn might even give some theological warrant, some religious support for this concession to my physical limitation.[1]

> "What a fellowship, what a joy divine,
> Leaning on the everlasting arms;
> What a blessedness, what a peace is mine,
> Leaning on the everlasting arms."

Although I may hold onto the pulpit, I am not, of course, actually "leaning" on it. And "leaning on the everlasting arms" of God's comfort and God's presence is something we all can do.

But you need not be concerned about whether I might be weaving a bit too much, or that I might possibly even lose my balance. I am fine with reading and preaching the Gospel right here, and I hope it is alright with you.

2

On the one hand, it is not a very big deal where the Gospel is read—so long as people can hear the words of promise. It is not a very big deal where the Gospel is read—so long as God's invitation to reconciliation can be heard.

It makes little difference where the Gospel Book is read, so long as people can hear the Gospel announcement of "redemption and release." The reading place is irrelevant, so long as everyone is reminded of Christ's gift of deep peace, and hears clearly the divine assurance of another chance.

On the other hand, the message our body posture and position give can say more than we might suppose. And our posture and position need to be consistent with the high value that faith finds in the Jesus story as the four New Testament Gospel writers have transmitted it to us.

For the Gospel is not just one tale among others. The Jesus story is the account of a human life divinely lived. It is the portrait of an other-regarding life that is posed as the model for our life. It is the narrative of a teacher who showed how one could become a neighbor to someone in need—the neglected, the ignored, and the forgotten ones of the world. The Gospel is the voice of God's most gracious generosity.

And so at its reading we may appropriately sign with the cross our head, our lips, and our heart. Such gestures consecrate our understanding, our speech, and our love to the one who consecrated his life and death for our saving. The Gospel story of his sacrifice then becomes the story of our own great relief.

The directions the Prayer Book gives for celebrating the Holy Eucharist reinforce this view, but in a more straightforward way:

"It is desirable that the Lessons be read from a lectern or pulpit, and that the Gospel be read from the same lectern, or from the pulpit, or from the midst of the congregation. It is desirable that the Lessons and the Gospel be read from a book or books of appropriate size and dignity." [BCP, p. 406]

3

The central issue in all of this is how best to honor the Gospel. The character of the book, the position of the reader, and our standing at its reading—all these are outward and quite visible signs of just such honoring.

We will honor the Gospel *Book* because we want to honor the Gospel *Story* as seriously as we can. And we will honor the Gospel *Story* because we want to honor and to be supported in our desire to live the Gospel *Life*.

And it is to that end that all our Gospel honoring tends: a life of compassion and company, a life of charity and service, a life of forgiveness and joy.

One of my professors put it this way: "While the Church has an utterance to make, sermons to preach, hymns to sing, and prayers to offer, above all it has a life to share. This life is God's free sharing of [God's] own self in Jesus Christ."[2]

NOTES

1. "Leaning on the Everlasting Arms," words by Elisha A. Hoffman, music by Anthony J. Showalter, 1887.
2. Julian N. Hartt, *Toward a Theology of Evangelism*, OR: Wpf and Stock; reprint, 2006, 117.

Part II

HOMILIES FOR THE SAKE OF HEAVEN

Chapter Four

In Ordinary Time

1. HEBREWS 12:1–2
"RUN"

1

The Epistle reading is very short—two verses, and all in one long sentence. Hear it once again:

"Therefore, since we are surrounded by so great a cloud of witnesses, let us also lay aside every weight and sin which clings so closely, and let us run with perseverance the race that is set before us, looking to Jesus the pioneer and perfecter of our faith, who for the joy that was set before him endured the cross, despising the shame, and is seated at the right hand of the throne of God." [Heb 12:1–2]

The writer counsels us to be true to our calling as Christ's blessed and empowered women and men, called to serve a grieving and fallen world. But more than that, these ancient words remind us not just how we might survive until our death, but also how we might move to the end of our days with some confidence. These are building-up words, and they provide us with the assurance that we really are supported by the powers of heaven in our effort to live faithfully, and in God's good time, to die unashamedly.

But there is a line in this very short Epistle reading that, although innocent enough, is troubling and hard for some of us to hear:

". . . let us *run* with perseverance the race that is set before us . . ." It is the invitation for us to *run* that gives me pause. And this directive is reinforced by a line in one of the Collects in which we pray that God might "grant that we may *run* without stumbling to obtain [God's] heavenly promises." [Collect for All Saints' Day] *Run without stumbling! Run with perseverance!*

Now I do not run any more, and I walk unaided with increasing difficulty. This decreasing mobility and problems of balance make it difficult for me to function any longer with the ease and confidence that I need, and that a congregation expects. And so I have informed the Senior Warden and the Bishop that I must bring my public ministry as a priest of the Church to a close at the end of the year.

2

So now back to the Epistle. Its plea that we might "run with perseverance" should come as no surprise to anyone who has listened carefully to the readings from the Bible for a while. For there is a lot of running in the Bible.

[1] Recall the rivalry between Jacob and Esau, the twin sons of Isaac. Jacob had tricked his brother Esau out of his birthright and blessing. In order to avoid Esau's great anger, Jacob had to flee the country. Many years later a meeting of the estranged brothers is arranged, and no one knows what might happen. The story-writer describes the outcome this way: "Esau *ran* to meet him and embraced him." [Gen 33:4] That is just the way how even long estrangements are healed.

[2] Recall Jesus' parable of the two sons [Lk 15:11–31]. One became a prodigal "wasting his substance in riotous living," and the other his hard-nosed, unforgiving brother. The bad boy has repented of his wasteful ways, and returns home. The Gospel writer describes his homecoming this way: "But while he was yet at a distance, his father saw him, and had compassion and *ran* and embraced him." That is what forgiveness always prompts us to do. That is the sign of just how impatient God is to welcome us home.

[3] Recall some of the Gospel accounts of the Day of Resurrection. In these reports everybody seems to be in a big hurry.

St. John tells it this way: "Now on the first day of the week Mary Magdalene came to the tomb early . . . and saw that the stone had been taken away from the tomb. So she *ran* and went to Simon Peter and the other disciple, the one whom Jesus loved. . . . Peter came out with the other disciple, and they went toward the tomb. They both *ran*." [Jn 20:1–3] That is what signs of new and eternal life do for people who are shut up in despair. Running now to spread the news. For if Christ be not raised, nothing else matters.

But notice that all of these passages simply describe people who are running, people who are in a great hurry. None of them really makes a claim on us. We might find these accounts interesting, but the picture of these people running is no threat to those of us who can run no longer, and who walk with some difficulty.

None of these stories, important as they are, supports the uncomfortable line in the Epistle: ". . . let us run with perseverance the race that is set before us . . ." Or the request in the Collect: "Grant that we may run without stumbling to obtain [God's] heavenly promises." In order to find that we have to turn to the Letters of St. Paul and to other documents that some early Christians wrote in his name.

He encouraged the Christians in Corinth with these words: "Do you not know that in a race all of the runners compete, but one receives the prize? So run that you may obtain it." [I Cor 9:24]

And he reminded the Christians in Philippi of his own great hope: I strive ". . . so that in the day of Christ I may be proud that I did not run in vain or labor in vain." [Phil 2:16]

But the happiest of all is the Epistle reading from the Letter to the Hebrews: "Let us run with perseverance the race that is set before us . . ." Obeying this request is a happy and glorious possibility for us because, as it says, "we are surrounded by so great a cloud of witnesses," cheering us on, encouraging us, urging us not to lose heart. This is that great company of the redeemed, who have already made it, and who are waiting for us. This is that great orchestra of praise, a vast choir of uncountable rejoicing and support.

3

The author of the Epistle is giving us a picture that might help us to think about the Christian life in an illuminating way—as a runner in an important race, who has a lot of help on the way from the sidelines, where the faithful already in glory are rooting for us.

But this picture of running a race may be a problem for those of us who no longer run and who might even walk with some difficulty. If so, we may take some comfort in the fact that the New Testament gives us many other images or pictures that can shed light on the meaning of the Christian life, from our birth to our death.

Some of them are no threat to those of us who are physically challenged, but others make us as uncomfortable as the call to run.

Some suggest that the Christian life is something like a journey or a pilgrimage—the life-long movement from our present house to our heavenly home. Others suggest more physical and more athletic pictures: The Christian life is a battle against the dark forces. "Fight the good fight," we are encouraged to do [I Tim 4:7], or "to take a stand" [Eph 6] against all those forces and people who threaten the serenity of those whose lives are served by God's grace.

Many pictures, but the same point is in them all: journey, pilgrimage, taking a stand, battle, fight, race.

If we reflect on our life in faith with any one of these pictures, we see that our movement from birth to death is not just one thing after another, but a passage with purpose, with direction.

If we reflect on our life in faith with any one of these pictures, we see that we are not just biding our time, but reaching out for the crown that those now in glory are holding out for us—the crown of victory!

If we keep this important Christian truth in mind, then those of us who no longer run or move with any speed, can take to heart the Epistle's invitation: "Therefore, since we are surrounded by so great a cloud of witnesses, let us also lay aide every weight and sin which clings so closely, and run with perseverance the race that is set before us."

2. MARK 14:45
"RANSOM"

1

Christians are called, and empowered by our baptism, to be imitators of Christ. His ministry of justice-making is to be our ministry. His mission of compassion-sharing is to be our mission. As God was in Christ—reconciling, healing, forgiving, so are we to be in all those places where God has led us and blest us to dwell—reconciling, healing, forgiving.

So it makes some difference what picture of Jesus we have in our minds as we go about our way of being Christ's agents in this indifferent and hostile world.

For his self-offering for the welfare of others is to be the model and the impetus for our self-offering for the wellbeing of others.

2

The picture Jesus' first followers most often used of him was simply *teacher*. And what a teacher he was!

Sometimes he taught in short, easily remembered sayings: "Blessed are the peacemakers, for they shall be called the children of God." [Mth 5:9]; "Where your treasure is, there will your heart be also." [Mth 6:21]

Sometimes he taught by telling stories. And some of the images in his stories are deeply embedded in our memories, where they can guide our hands and feet as we try to do the right thing. Consider these pictures:

- A prodigal son and his churlish brother, reminding us of how impatient God is to forgive.
- A helpful Samaritan, reminding us to become a neighbor, instead of worrying about who our neighbor is.
- Rain falling on the just and unjust alike, reassuring us that the generosity of heaven has no favorites.
- Jesus inviting us to "consider the lilies of the field, how they grow," calling us to accept the grace that surrounds us all the time, without our asking.
- Jesus' commending a widow who gives her mite—her last small coin—to the Temple, and in doing so he indicts and challenges all the systems that exploit the most vulnerable, and fleece them of their meager resources.
- A woman searching for a lost coin, a shepherd searching for a lost sheep, comforting us with the certain knowledge of God's ability to find us no matter how far we may have strayed.

All of these teaching pictures can help us understand what God expects of us in our dealings with one another. All these images can help us learn how extravagant is the cascade of compassion that God showers on us.

The disciples themselves were just learners too, until the very end. It is only on the very last page of Matthew's Gospel that Jesus finally authorizes the disciples to become teachers themselves.

"Jesus came and said to them, 'Go . . . and make disciples of all nations . . . teaching them to observe all that I have commanded you.'" [Mth28:20]

Ever since then, we who bear his name have tried, by word or by example, to heed this command, and to become teachers of his vision of the lavish generosity of God.

3

Another picture Jesus' disciples soon came to use when they spoke about Jesus was *lord*. All the more remarkable for those early Jewish Christians, since "lord" was the word they used when they spoke to or about God. They called Jesus "lord" for they had begun to recognize him as the human face of the divine. And what a lord he was!

Jesus redefined what it means to be a lord. He was not a lord of infinite power, but a lord who emptied himself, who set aside divine prerogatives. Not a remote, highhanded lord, but a lord of great condescension. He was a lord with no subjects, only followers he preferred to call "friends." Not a lord to keep us obedient, but a lord who chooses to be our companion in suffering and need. Not a lord who worries about holding onto power, but a lord who gives it away.

St. Paul wrote this about the new kind of lord Jesus was, to the Christians in Philippi: "Let this mind be in you that was in Christ Jesus; who though he was in the form of God, did not count equality with God a thing to be grasped, but emptied himself, taking the form of a servant . . ." [Phil 2:5,6]

If we will, we can teach Jesus' message, and we can try to have in us the same mind that was in this self-emptying, other-regarding Lord. If we will, his way of being teacher and lord can be a model for us, as we learn to live by the words early Christians used when they talked about Jesus.

4

But how did Jesus talk about himself? How did Jesus understand himself? What pictures did he use when he reflected on his own life?

The oldest of the Gospels—Matthew, Mark, and Luke—are not going to be much help. In these Gospels Jesus rarely talked about himself at all.

But something very different emerges in the Gospel of John. Here Jesus talks about himself a lot. He uses many images to interpret the meaning of his ministry for his disciples and for us. He gave a now familiar list of self-naming pictures. These are words that have brought great comfort and reassurance to believing women and men across the centuries:

Jesus said: "I am the bread of life." [Jn 6:35]. "I am the light of the world." [Jn 8:12]. "I am the door of the sheep." [Jn 10:9]. "I am the good shepherd." [Jn 10:11] "I am the true vine." [Jn 15:1] "I am the way, the truth, and the life." [Jn 14:6] "I am the resurrection and the life." [Jn 11:25]

These pictures may not tell us very much about what we ought to be up and doing in our work for the kingdom. But they do point to the great saving effect that Jesus has wrought on our behalf.

5

Consider now the rare Jesus' self-reflective talk in St. Mark's Gospel [Mk 10:35–45]. For the very first time in this Gospel, Jesus publicly interprets the meaning of his life and mission. In doing so, he uses the strange word "ransom." "The Son of Man came not to be served, but to serve, and to give his life as a *ransom* for many." [Mk 14:45]

Now we can understand "teacher," lord," shepherd." But what are we to make of the notion of Jesus as "ransom?" What is Jesus saying about himself, with this word "ransom," and what does this "ransom" teaching have to do with our life and work?

As we know, "ransom" sets someone free who has been held against their will. And that, says Jesus, is what he came to do—set people free. That is what forgiveness does. And that is what the Gospel is all about: "You are forgiven." Nothing more, nothing less. And this is what the eternal priesthood of the Church is authorized to announce in Christ's name.

We are ransomed people, set free from an obsession with ourselves so that we may be genuinely open to the other. We are ransomed people, set free from having our lives determined by our past mistakes. We are ransomed people, given a second chance. We are ransomed people, free to start the day afresh.

And so we can talk about Jesus as "teacher," as "lord," and as "ransom."

But we will not do so just to admire, but to imitate. Not just to honor, but to pursue. Not just to praise, but to adhere. Not just to endorse, but to follow.

For in this Holy Eucharist, Christ is not a dead leader whom we remember, but a lively counselor whom we make really present again.

We do not just have memories of Jesus, we keep him from perishing—as we embody and carry forth the mission of this teacher, this lord, this ransom-giver, in a sick and grieving world.

3. JOHN 6:24–35
"I AM THE BREAD OF LIFE"

1

Christian faith and life, as we experience it in the Anglican Tradition, is shaped and nourished by three books—The Book of Common Prayer, the Hymnal, and the Bible. They help us pray, to praise, and to profess. I look with special interest today to the Bible.

The Bible is not so much a book, as it is a collection or an anthology of many different pieces—66 in fact. And this is without counting the books of *The Apocrypha*. These are those other ancient texts that the Episcopal Church reads, attends to, and honors in various ways. These writings were gathered from many ancient Hebrew and early Christian sources. When we put them all together, we actually have a small library bound up as a book.

Fortunately, there is much in that anthology that we can safely ignore—battle strategies, court records, lists of kings and enemies, arrangements for slaves, endorsements of polygamy and male domination.

But many biblical passages call for our serious attention, for they can so deeply nourish our growth in grace.

[1] There are *reprimands* here that we do well to heed, if we want to clothe our lives with amendment and charity. Many of these were first voiced by the Old Testament prophets, for they were the conscience, the social critics of the ancient Hebrews. They regularly denounced the failure of the people and their leaders to abide by God's expectation.

Amos was especially high on reprimands. He inveighed against the blind, short-sighted, self-indulgence of the people and their leaders. He condemns them with the memorable cry of judgment and lament that has indicted false security and religious hypocrisy ever since:

"Woe to those who are at ease in Zion." [Amos 6:1] That is a reprimand to heed.

[2] There are *promises* here that we do well to embrace, if we want to face the terrible with resolve when it comes. The promises of Christ can be a source of great comfort and assurance as we keep on keeping on in the best way we can.

- I think of the very last words Jesus spoke to the disciples in St. Matthew's Gospel. At the Gospel's beginning God's messenger announces that Mary's Son will be "Emmanuel" ["God with us"]. [Mth 2:23] And now at the end the promise is fulfilled as Jesus says, "Lo, I am with you always." [Mth 28:20] Because of that promise, we need never fear the future.
- I think of the security he pledges for the ongoing life of the believing community: "Where two or three are gathered in my name, there am I in the midst of them." [Mth 18:20]. Because of that promise we know that even if we "do not agree on much of anything" we "can still care for one another through almost everything," [Barbara Brown Taylor][1], thanks to the ministering presence of Christ in our midst
- I think especially of his warm words of welcome that give serenity to the ending of our life: "In my Father's house are many mansions. . . . I go to prepare a place for you" [Jn 14:2] Because of that promise we can move into whatever future God has for us with solace and trust. We know that all will be well, in the words of the old Gospel hymn, if we are "standing on the promises of God."

[3] There are *moral counsels* here that we do well to heed, if we want to conform our lives to the blessed permissions of the Gospel.

- Jesus had little use for what we once called the "pomp and vainglory of the world," and suggested a standard more befitting those whom God has loved into life:

"Consider the lilies of the field, how they grow. They toil not, neither do they spin, yet Solomon in all his glory was not arrayed like one of these." [Mth 6:28–29]

Such a regard for even the flowers might lead us to place more confidence in the care of God that surrounds us all the time

- I think of St. Paul's advice for all those in a church discussion, who are tempted to seek advantage over justice, and to pursue victory in the debate at any cost. In his Epistle to the Ephesians we hear his cautionary word to all those who dispute with one another:

"Speak the truth in love." [Eph. 4:16] Heeding this counsel might preserve believers' camaraderie with one another, in a bond of peace.

[4] There are *encouragements* here that we do well to embrace, if we want to be free from the face of anxiety.

The ancient Hebrew poet, who first sang the psalms, knew so boldly that walking even through the valley of the shadow of death is not a journey into unrelieved darkness:

"The Lord is my shepherd, I shall not want. . . . He restores my soul." [Ps 23:1,2]

2

There are *declarations* here that endorse, verify, and confirm all of the other upbuilding discoveries in Holy Scripture.

I think of Jesus' self-identification in last Sunday's Gospel [Mk 6:45–52] He gives his reassuring words in a storm at sea to embolden passengers, then and now, who brave tempest of any sort far from land:"

"Take heart. It is I. Do not be afraid."

The King James translators put his blessed comfort this way: "Be of good cheer. It is I. Be not afraid."

Before long, the disciples' terror will turn to veneration; their panic will change to reverence.

The Greek text of St. Matthew's story gives us an important clue. Coming to the disciples in their storm-tossed boat, Jesus says, "It is I." [in Greek, *ego eimi*]. In the Old Testament, this is the name of God disclosed to Moses—the great "I am." [Ex 13:14]

And so for St. Matthew's readers, the calming presence of those fearsome waves is the very instance of the upholding, everlasting arms of God.

And so St. Matthew's story resolves the problem of Jonah. Jonah is cast into the sea by sailors who are so terrified of the high waves that they tried to calm the story by ridding their boat of their strange passenger.

The reverse happens with Jesus and his disciples. When Jesus comes on board, and becomes a passenger along with them, the wind calms down "Take heart," he said. "Be of good cheer. It is I. Do not be afraid."

3

I think, at last, of the dramatic declaration in today's Gospel [Jn 6:24–35], an announcement that clarifies and endorses our interest in the saving words of the Bible.

When Jesus declares "I am the Bread of Life," he opens a gallery of seven wondrous windows into his sacred identity, seven shining pictures of the One who secures our healing and our eternal rescue. These images endorse everything in the Bible that sustains and guides us—the reprimands and promises, the moral counsels and encouragements.

These "I AM" sayings authorize our belief. They certify our most serious hope. And they warm our hearts against the cold suspicion of our disbelieving neighbors.

Taking them to heart enables us to follow St. Paul's hope for the Ephesians, and for us as well, that we might "come to the measure of the full stature of Christ," and thus avoid being "tossed to and fro and blown about by every wind of doctrine." [Eph 4:13,14]

Hear the precious words once again. Jesus said:
"I am the Bread of Life." [Jn 6:33]
"I am the Light of the World." [Jn 8:12]
"I am the Door for the Sheep. [Jn 10:17]
"I am the Good Shepherd." [Jn 10:11]
"I am the Resurrection and the Life." [Jn 11:25]
"I am the Way, the Truth, and the Life." [Jn 14:6]
"I am the True Vine.'" [Jn 15:1]

You will notice that the envelope of these sayings that St. John has preserved and transmitted to us is the Holy Eucharist. In this act of eating and drinking in his Name, we receive what St. Ignatius, at the beginning of the second century, called "the medicine of immortality."[2]

The Bread of Life and the True Vine—bread and wine, the Body and Blood of Christ. We do not share this just to keep the memory of Christ alive, but to join our lives to his, and feast on his saving presence among us. At this altar, hunger and thirst will be no more.

He bids us eat and drink together. This is an invitation and a promise by which we can live, and live eternally.

4. COLLECT FOR PROPER 28[3]
"THE SUN OF RIGHTEOUSNESS"

1

The Collect for today is one of the finest Collects in the entire Prayer Book. In this Collect we prayed for God to help us to pay serious attention to the Holy Scriptures: "Grant us [so] to hear them, read, mark, learn, and inwardly digest them."

When I was younger, indeed, very much younger, I thought that the Collect was authorizing and urging us to mark up our Bibles—underlining important and memorable passages with a red pencil or a yellow highlighter; putting question marks or exclamation marks in the margins, alongside puzzles or surprising words: "read, *mark*, learn," we prayed, "and inwardly digest."

But Thomas Cranmer, the 16th century author of the Collect and the architect of much of the *Book of Common Prayer,* had something else, and something much simpler in mind. To ask that we might "read, . . . , learn, and inwardly digest" and be nourished by the Holy Scriptures is pretty clear. But what it means to "mark" the Bible is not so obvious. Bishop Cranmer clearly did not mean that we are to "mark up," our Bible—to underline, or to make notes, or pen comments in the margins.

To "mark," as the Collect invites us to do, is simply to pay serious attention to these Scriptures. To "mark" the biblical word in this way is to heed its admonitions, to delight in its assurances, to be chastened by its warnings.

To "mark" the biblical work in this way is to be informed by its wisdom, and to give thanks for the advent of him in whom all the signposts, all the promises, all the hopes, all the releases find their fulfillment—Jesus of Nazareth, the human face of God.

You will remember that St. John's Gospel speaks of Jesus as God's Word: "In the beginning was the Word, and the Word was with God, and the Word was God." [Jn 1:1] St. John wants to say that Jesus is God's Word because he is the one in whom God has expressed himself in the clearest way. It is as if the Bible itself is anticipating today's Collect, and saying to us, "Mark my Word!"

2

And, of course, there is a lot of that Word in our service that we regularly *read* and *learn*. This means that each week we are reminded, reprimanded, and nourished by God's great permissions and beatitudes that this book contains. This means that each week we are sustained by its blessings remembered and benefits forgotten, and comforted always by the divine promise that "All will be well. All will be well."

In the Eucharistic liturgy there is always one of the Psalms to say or sing, many of which were songs sung in the great Jerusalem Temple. The Psalm is preceded by a reading from the Old Testament, the religious literature of the ancient Israelites—their prophets, lawgivers, poets and story-tellers. Then follows a selection from one of the letters or epistles from St. Paul or St. John that were passed around and shared among the early Christians meeting in their house churches. And finally, with special honor, a passage from one of the four New Testament Gospels—the sayings and deeds of Jesus of Nazareth, God's supreme agent.

We will *mark* the Bible's words, for they point us to the truth about how to live most fully in this fallen world. They disclose what is amiss in our life, what of the world God has made that we have marred, and what God has done in the life of the whole Christ to mend it finally and with great charity.

3

The prophet Malachi, whom we heard in the Old Testament reading, pointed poetically to this when he assured his readers, in a rather strange picture, that ". . . the sun of righteousness shall rise with healing in its wings." [Mal 4:2]

Malachi's promise is the very last voice of the Old Testament. He promises the advent or the coming of a new, saving act of God. The story of that surprising turn of events takes us to the life of Jesus of Nazareth, and to the pages of the New Testament.

But Malachi's hopeful vision is not the last voice of the Hebrew Scriptures. The Jewish Bible and the Christian Old Testament contain much of the same material, but the two books arrange these texts differently. And this means that they end up being two quite different books.

The Jewish Bible does not end with the forward-looking prophets, such as Malachi. The Jewish Bible ends with II Chronicles. Here the Persian ruler, Cyrus, allows the exiled Judeans, now living in Babylon, to return to Judea; to rebuild the Temple in Jerusalem, and to reinstitute the Torah or the Law of Moses as their national constitution. And so the Hebrew Scriptures or the

Jewish Bible ends by pointing to a return to the original beginning under the Law, urging the community to try again to renew its national life lived through the Law.

The arrangement of the Christian Old Testament is very different. This book ends with Malachi's prophecy. He anticipates a new divine act, not a return to a vision of the people living under the Law. Christians have recognized this new act in the teachings and deeds and person of Jesus Christ, and have continued to live and to hope by its power.

For what Jesus brings is more permission than Law, more example than command, more welcome than restrictions. He wants to be more companion than ruler. And that is what we have always needed, and what we have always found in Christ:

Not more information, but release from our mistakes. Not more laws to increase our guilt, but the assurance that we are so forgiven that we can become forgivers. Not some new privilege, but the glory of knowing that each one of us is already a child of God.

4

This is the great healing with whose wings Malachi envisions the "sun of righteousness" to rise. When Malachi speaks of this advent as a new coming of the sun, he is drawing on one of the most familiar symbols of the divine in the ancient Near East. And one of the Psalms speaks of God as a "sun and shield." [Ps 84:11]

But like all symbols for God taken from nature, the "sun" is ambiguous. It brings warmth and heat without which nothing can grow, but it can also make deserts and bring drought and famine.

So Malachi is making a bold move when he links the rising of the sun to the dawning of a new saving age in human history.

For this reason early Christian writers identified Malachi's "sun" of righteousness [s u n], the life-supporting center of the universe, with Jesus Christ, God's "Son" [s o n].

We will soon attend to his advent, but not with anxiety or great worry, nor by fretting about some divine time-table. For we already live by his grace that empowers us every day. We already experience his coming, his advent, in every Eucharist, in every gesture of acceptance that we either give or receive.

We will read and learn from the Holy Scriptures. When the Holy Spirit says in that reading and in that learning, "Mark my Word," we can come to a great rest, for we will have been fed with the imperishable Bread of Heaven.

We will read and learn from the Holy Scriptures. When the Holy Spirit says in that reading and in that learning, "Mark my Word," we will begin to realize that there is no darkness so deep that is not illumined by the "Son of Righteousness" who has risen "with healing in his wings."

5. COLLECT FOR PROPER 28[4]
"INWARDLY DIGESTING HOLY SCRIPTURE"

1

The Collect bids us attend to the Holy Scriptures in special ways. We have just prayed that we might "read, mark, learn, and inwardly digest" the life-enhancing power of these ancient words. If we do this, we can hear God calling us to a life-policy of caring. The Scriptures are full of poems and stories, dreams and proclamations, that point us to the truth about how best to live in this fallen world They hold up a mirror before us so that we may see what is amiss in our life, and how the cracks in our life might be mended.

These holy texts reveal what God has done and continues to do to remedy our plight. They remind us each week of what God has done and continues to do to cure our deepest needs.

We hear these ancient words not just to refresh our memories, as wonderful and important as such a recollection might be. We listen to them so that they might feed our hearts and spur our wills. The Collect of the Day invites us to attend to the Holy Scriptures in just that special way. We are bidden not just to "read, mark, and learn," but also to "inwardly digest them."

Here in the Bible are stories and pictures, commands and promises, reprimands and allowances—all to nourish our growth in grace. If we listen carefully week-by-week, we can hear these old words addressing some moments of our most serious wants.

In this sermon I want to suggest something of what our life might be like, were we to heed the Collect's urging, not just to "read, mark, and learn," but to "inwardly digest" the words of Scripture.

To "inwardly digest" means being sustained by what is life-giving in these venerable words, but it also means setting aside whatever is of less value because it is bound to the people and the time and place from whence it has come. [as it is the case with the readings appointed for today!] As in a normal digestive process, we are fed by the true nutrients, but we expel what is not digestible.

2

[1] When we wonder just what the divine intention is for our life, so beset as it is with the struggle for control and deference, we could recall the picture of the man and the woman in the Garden of Eden. In that primeval paradise, mutuality is God's design. In Eden, partnership, not control or domination of one by the other, is the divine design.

"So God created humankind in his image . . . male and female he created them . . ." [Gen 1:27] No domination, no submission, no control here, only mutuality. Until it is spoiled by sin.

[2] When we wonder if the way we have messed things up might put us beyond God's willingness to forgive, we could recall Jesus' picture of the eager father, who runs out down the road to welcome home his prodigal son, still a long way off.

"Bring forth the best robe and put it on him. And let us eat and be merry; for this son of mine was dead and is alive again; he was lost and is found!" [Lk 15:22–24]

Or we could recall Jesus' gracious words to the woman accused of adultery, as the man who was responsible for the deed got away:

"Neither do I condemn you. Go your way, and sin no more."[Jn 8:11]

[3] When we wonder just how to respond to the scarred and the wounded of the world, when we wonder just how to care for those for whom God cares, we could recall Jesus' picture of the traveler from Samaria, who saw to the misery of an enemy alien when his own countrymen avoided him but whose plight claimed his help:

"A man was going down from Jerusalem to Jericho, and fell into the hands of robbers, who stripped him, beat him and went away, leaving him half dead. A Samaritan while traveling came near him; and when he saw him he was moved with compassion. He went to him and bandaged his wounds . . . Go, and do likewise." [Lk 10:30, 33–34, 37]

[4] When we worry if we are presenting ourselves to others in just the right way, we could recall one of Jesus' loveliest pictures:

"Consider the lilies of the field, how they grow. They toil not, neither do they spin, yet Solomon in all his glory was not arrayed like one of them . . ." [Mth 6:28–29]

[5] When we wonder about what lies beyond the time and space God has given us on the earth, we could recall the pictures in Jesus' promise:

"In my Father's house are many mansions. . . . And I go to prepare a place for you." [Jn 14:1, 8]

[6] Whenever we feel that we have it made, and know for sure that God is on our side, we should recall the words of the prophet Amos:

"Woe to those who are at ease in Zion!" [Amos 6:1]

[7] Whenever life seems to be out of joint, whenever all that we know and cherish seems to crumble, or when we seem to be having too hard a time, then we could recall the Psalmist's words:

". . . underneath are the everlasting arms." [Deut 33:27]

Or this: "They that sow in tears shall reap in joy." [Ps 126:5]

3

If we have truly been nourished by what of Scripture we have been able inwardly to digest, many moments of our life will be blessed.

[1] Instead of "so long," or "have a nice day," our leave-taking might sometimes be informed by the more ancient words: "The Lord watch between me and thee when we are absent one from the other." [Gen 32:40]

[2] If we are at a loss to find words that can shape our love for another, we might recall the widowed Ruth's moving plea that bound her to her mother-in-law Naomi:

"Entreat me not to leave you, or to return from following after you; for where you go I will go, and where you lodge I will lodge; your people shall be my people. And your God my God; where you die, I will die; and there will I be buried." [Ruth 2:15–17]

[3] If we have forgotten what God expects of us, we should reclaim Micah's announcement:

"He has showed you . . . what is good; and what does the Lord require of you but to do justice, and to love kindness, and to walk humbly with your God?" [Micah 6:8]

[4] If we are ever puzzled about what the proper goal of our social and political life should be, we can call to remembrance Amos' shattering plea:

[God says]" "Take away from me the noise of your songs, to the melody of your harps I will not listen. But let justice roll down like waters, and righteousness like an ever-flowing stream." [Amos 5:23–25]

Or the claim in St. Peter's sermon: "I truly understand that God shows no partiality, but in every nation anyone who fears him and does what is right is acceptable to him." [Acts 10:34–35]

[5] If the life of the Gospel and the mission of the Church are ever in doubt, we can recall St. Paul's commendation:

"There is no longer Jew or Greek, there is no longer slave or free, there is no longer male or female, for all of you are one in Christ Jesus." [Gal 3:28]

[Because] "Anyone who is in Christ is a new creation." [II Cor 5:17]

4

That is something of what our life might be like when we pray the Collect of the Day with utmost seriousness.

None of these holy words is a proof-text to help us win an argument. But each one is a comment to nudge us to a life of holiness, to let the seeds of grace grow.

We do not "read, mark, learn, and inwardly digest" these life-giving words of Holy Scripture in order to recover a lost time of virtue. But we will do as the Collect invites us, so that "we may embrace and ever hold fast the blessed hope of everlasting life" that God has given us in our Savior Jesus Christ.

6. PSALM 34:8
"TASTING GOD"

1

We gather here in company with one another, and by this pulpit and lectern and altar, for many different reasons:

- to praise God for the lavish grace that surrounds us every day; to receive anew the forgiveness that opens doors and windows for us, just when we thought we would never have another chance;
- to be reminded that we are the stewards of the offerings of generations of women and men who worked and prayed before us in this sacred space.

We gather to remember who we are as the people of God, charged with a mission for human dignity;

- to be nourished by him who is the True Vine and the Bread of Life, the very medicine of immortality;

We gather to learn afresh what it means to be faithful agents of God's kingdom in a hostile and indifferent world;

- to receive the law of love newly enjoined upon our hearts;

We gather to find but more encouragement as we seek to be gratefully and responsibly present to all the people with whom our lives are bound.

Whether we come by habit or conscience, we are helped in this endeavor by what we hear and see, by what we do and share. Sometimes it may be the words of Scripture that make the difference. For these ancient texts can sometimes shed a happy light on our effort to embrace a life policy of caring.

The Bible sends us stories and pictures, dreams and admonitions that can convince and empower us to be for one another in ways we could not have imagined. And there is a lot to choose from.

The preacher is most often constrained by something in the Gospel appointed for the day, less frequently by a line in the Epistle or Old Testament reading, but rarely from the Psalm.

2

In all my years at one pulpit or another in various parishes in this diocese, I have probably not preached more than a dozen times on a text, on a picture or a line from one of the Psalms. That is rather surprising.

For a Psalm, in whole or in part, is said or sung at every service. And the Psalter, the collection of these 150 poems, is a very large part, 225 pages, in the Prayer Book.

But it is easier to comment on a story or a letter than to interpret a poem. The Epistles and the Gospels seem so readily accessible, but the poetry of the Psalms often seems so puzzling and obscure.

One can hardly be blamed, then, for preferring to talk about The Prodigal Son, the Good Samaritan, or St. Paul's acknowledgement that "faith, hope, and love abide . . . but the greatest of these is love." That seems far more important than deciphering what the Psalmist had in mind by inviting us to "Worship the Lord in the beauty or holiness" [Ps 96:9], or to ask us to join in affirming "How lovely is thy dwelling place, O Lord of hosts." [Ps 84:1], although both of those lines are precious to me.

All of that having been said, however, there are such treasures in the Psalms that the Gospels and Epistles, the stories and the admonitions of the other appointed lessons can occasionally and safely be set aside for a day.

But one must be careful with the Psalms. For they speak not only of trust and compassion, not only of forgiveness and thanksgiving. But sometimes they also speak in dreadful ways of a wrathful and angry God, of wreaking vengeance on one's enemies, of hostile deeds against all who oppose God's chosen ones. All this is the voice of terror, the prayers of tribal religion, and are unworthy of our serious attention. Fortunately those primitive parts of these otherwise quite wonderful poems are left out when we sing or say them, and are properly left in the dust bins of misdirected prayers.

But what holy words we are left with, words that can shape and shore up our tries to survive with some peace and equanimity. What holy words we are left with, words that help support our efforts to do the best we can, when the unexpected happens. Here are a few lines from the Psalms that we ought to hear again and to hold onto if we can.

3

"They that sow in tears shall reap in joy. He that goeth forth and weepeth, bearing precious seed, shall doubtless come again rejoicing, bringing his sheaves with him." [Ps 126:5, 6 {KJV}]

As is the case with many of the Psalms, this one draws on agricultural imagery—sowing seed and reaping the harvest; the hard, sometimes tearful work of readying the ground, planting and cultivating the crops, but also giving thanks for a plentiful harvest.

But this rhythm of the farm—sowing and harvesting, weeping and rejoicing—is not peculiar to an agricultural life. It is the common human experience of needing to deal with what is at hand, and, at the same time, keeping an eye on the promise. This is the pattern of the faithful life:

- facing the difficult, all the while, counting on the constant presence of God to uphold and sustain;
- tending to the necessary matters of the present time, all the while knowing that there awaits a crown of glory;
- managing the demands of the day, all the while resting assured that God will bring some healing on the morrow.

"They that sow in tears shall reap in joy."
And there are other wise and welcome words in the Psalms.
The Psalmist believed that the ordinary world of human deeds and hopes is truly the fit place where God's glory and human efforts are honored. And so he wrote: "What if I had not believed that I should see the goodness of the Lord in the land of the living." [Ps 27:17] And in another place he said: "The needy shall not always be forgotten, and the hope of the poor shall not perish forever." [Ps 9:18]

The Psalmist understood the frailty of human life, and how precious are the days and years that God has given us; he knew that there are loves to be shared and cares to be taken before we die. And so he wrote: "Lord, make me to know the measure of my days on earth." [Ps 29:47]

But of the several things we are invited or encouraged or directed to do in the Psalms, the command we hear most often is the plea for us to be thankful.

"O give thanks to the Lord, for he is gracious, and his mercy endures forever." [Ps 136:1] "It is a good thing to give thanks to the Lord." [Ps 92:1]

When we give thanks, we are admitting that we are not self-sufficient. When we give thanks, we are confessing our need for others.

When we give thanks, we recognize just how gifted our lives have been.

When we give thanks, we own that we are the recipients of a grace beyond our imagining, and beyond our counting.

One of the monastic blessings at table points out the divine donor of the bread and cheese and wine about to be consumed, and then adds one request: "Give us a grateful heart, O God."

4

I turn finally to one of the most unusual of the ancient appeals in the Psalms, the very strange invitation in Psalm 34: to "Taste and see that the Lord is good." [Ps 34:8] *"Taste* and *see* . . ."[5]

He invites us to set aside doctrines and theologies for a time, and sense God with all the aspects of our bodily existence. Trusting God is not an intellectual matter, but an issue of the heart. The Psalmist asks us to be open to God with every power that we have.

It is no surprise that this Psalm was often paired in the early Church with the stories of Jesus' feeding the multitudes, and with Jesus' self-identification in St. John's Gospel as the "Bread of Life."

The Psalmist urges us to "taste and see that the Lord is good." And his appeal is given special meaning with the Eucharistic invitation to eat and drink of the broken and outpoured life of Christ: "The gifts of God for the people of God. Take them in remembrance that Christ died for you, and *feed* on him in your hearts with thanksgiving."

We do not accept the invitation of the Psalmist to be reminded of the self-offering of Christ on our behalf, but to refresh his presence among us.

We do not "break bread together" to pay our respects to a departed leader who met an untimely death, but to join our lives to his, and to pray that he will endow our efforts to do the best we can with his counsel and his recovering grace.

We do not receive the Holy Communion just to recall the sacrifice once made for us, but to have our conscience informed by his sacrifice, to have our spirits nourished by the showering cascade of his compassion, and to have our sympathies deepened by his most holy example.

"Taste and see that the Lord is good."

7. JOHN 6:52–58
"COMPANIONS AND CRITICS OF CHRIST"

1

Jesus had both companions and critics. He had friends and followers from the beginning of his public life. He also had adversaries as well, who opposed his work from the beginning.

The very words and deeds that attracted and endeared him to so many, were the very same words and deeds that irritated and offended so many others. One reason may be his willingness to put the wellbeing of persons over obedience to the letter of the Law. And those who saw themselves as "guardians of the Law" had a hard time with that attitude, even as their modern-day successors still do. Evidence of this attitude is all through the Gospels:

Once Jesus allowed his disciples to pick grain on the Sabbath Day, thus working when working is forbidden. They must have been hungry! He was soon criticized for that. But his response showed that this very religious Jew valued the enhancement of human life over literal adherence to the Law. "The Sabbath was made for man," he said, "not man for the Sabbath." [Mk 2:27]

Hospitality and social justice were more important to him than ethnic loyalty. So he said to Zacchaeus the tax collector, who was watching him from way up in a sycamore tree, "Make haste and come down, for I must stay at your house today." [Lk 9:1–10]

And to the bewilderment of some of his co-religionists, [to use a quaint word from the King James Version], Jesus quickly got the reputation of being, a "drunkard and a wine-bibber." [Lk 7:34] His disciples were asked over and over, "Why does he eat with tax collectors and sinners?" [Mk 2:16]. And in St. John's account of his attending the wedding at Cana in Galilee, we discover that Jesus was able to provide some really good wine for the assembled guests after what the caterer provided had run out. [Jn 2:1–11]

Yet for all this support and against all this hostility, the life he lived was the life he chose.

This part of the Gospel story tells us something about religious conflict and possibility in first century Palestine. But it also names the hope that all of Christ's present companions share. For our interest is not in just getting the history straight, but in finding energy so that we can start up again. Our interest is in having our resolve to care for the other and to do the just thing strengthened beyond our personal habits.

2

The Collect for Proper 15 sums it up well. In that prayer, we acknowledged that God's Son is given to us as "an example of godly life," and then we asked for grace so that we might "follow daily in the blessed steps of his most holy life."

The New Testament Gospels report that his companions sought to do just that. But being a companion of Christ was no easier in first century Palestine than it is now in this place.

The experience of Jesus' early supporters and friends was not very different from our own. They found their lives wonderfully changed by his presence with them. And so do we. His circle of agents and envoys of his grace to a broken world, realized that they had been given important life-saving things to do. And so do we. They rejoiced that they had been gathered into an unpredictable family of believers of all sorts, where they need not think alike, so long as they cared for one another without question, and without hesitance. And so do we.

But for all that intimacy, some of his disciples and devotees just did not get it! They knew they needed to be with Jesus. They sensed a new direction for their lives because of him. But they so often misunderstood him and his vision for a new humanity, right up until the very end. Perhaps they were so bound up with the old ways. Or perhaps Jesus' dream of a compassion shared, and a bundle of sins so generously forgiven was so startlingly different from anything they had ever known, that they had a hard time grasping it. Was it really possible that God could wipe the slate clean? Would God really throw away the account books?

But at least the Gospel writers were honest enough to tell us all about their limitations, the confusion of Jesus' early supporters and advocates. They made no attempt to cover up the heavy-headedness of the disciples.

St. Luke tells this story. Jesus is reminding his disciples that what he has been doing and saying is likely to lead to his death. And the very next sentence is this: "And an argument arose among them as to which of them was the greatest." [Lk 9:46]

Again, as Jesus breaks bread and pours out wine during his last supper with his friends, he says that this is really his life about to be broken and poured out for our saving in his soon death. And the very next sentence is this: "A dispute arose among them, which of them was to be regarded as the greatest." [Lk 22:24]

In the "kingdom of equals" that Jesus' self-offering creates and to which his supreme neighborliness invites us, there are no "places of honor;" there is no "which of us is the greatest!"

If we remember this, we should not be discouraged when we are confused about life in the Kingdom of God. We should not be upset when we are uncertain and puzzled about the mandates of the Gospel. We are in the good company of all those who from the beginning were confused. We may indeed love the Gospel and Jesus who gives it voice, and we may aim to live, and live up to the Gospel life to which he invites and fashions for us. But we still, like his first company of saints, all love imperfectly. And Jesus says "That's alright!" We are not called to be perfect, only to be as faithful as we can.

3

Jesus' companions may have been slow in understanding what Jesus said and did and who he really was, but Jesus' critics knew full well what was happening before their eyes. They were incensed by what they heard about this "stranger from Galilee," and by what they saw him doing, and by what he said about himself. The catalogue of horrors his enemies drew up is long. Here are a few entries:

[a] Once some men were carrying a paralyzed friend on a pallet, trying to get him close to Jesus. [Mk 2:5–11] But the building was so crowded that they had to remove part of the roof and then let the stretcher down through the opening. St. Mark then reports that "when Jesus saw their faith, he said to the paralytic, 'My son, your sins are forgiven.'" But some scribes sitting nearby protested: "Why does this man speak thus? It is blasphemy! Who can forgive sins, but God alone?" Jesus answered them by asking, "Which is easier, to say to the paralytic, 'Your sins are forgiven,'" or to say, 'Rise, take up your pallet and walk'? But that you may know that the Son of Man has authority on earth to forgive sins—he said to the paralytic, 'I say to you, rise, take up your pallet and go home.' And he rose, and immediately took up the pallet, and went out before them all.'"

[b] When Jesus enters Jerusalem at the beginning of the last week of his life, he goes to the mount of the great Jerusalem Temple. There on one of the plazas, dealers were changing money for the pilgrims who had come to town, so that they might have proper coinage to buy animals to offer for sacrifice. Jesus is enraged, overturns their tables, whips them and drives them out, and cries: "My house shall be called the house of prayer; but you have made it a den of thieves." [Mth 21:13] That halted, at least for the day, the elaborate rituals that made the Temple a bloody place indeed. But symbolically, his action challenged the whole system of killing animals to worship God.[6]

[c] In St. John's Gospel, Jesus speaks of himself in ways that his critics simply could not countenance. His words there identified the authority by

which he forgave sins and cleansed the Temple. "The Father and I are one," he said. [Jn 10:30]. "He who has seen me has seen the Father." [Jn 14:9] His angry adversaries were about to stone him. They said, "It is not for a good work that we stone you, but for blasphemy; because you, being a man, make yourself Go" [Jn 10:33]

[d] But very high on the list of Jesus' troubling and offensive announcements was the revelation and the invitation in today's Gospel [Jn 6:52–58]: "Those who eat my flesh and drink my blood have eternal life, and I will raise them up on the last day.... Those who eat my flesh and drink my blood abide in me, and I in them."

But it would have been impossible for a religiously observant Jew to contemplate violating the so-called kosher rules—with an absolute prohibition against eating flesh from which blood had not been drained. Doing so would not only have broken a dietary rule, it would have separated oneself from the Jewish community. But what they abhorred is precisely what keeps giving us life.

Perhaps it was the extravagance of the metaphor Jesus used ["body" and "blood"] that so offended his literal-minded critics. But as my priestly friend Barbara Crafton reminds us, Jesus' poetic language has given us "a way of sharing his life and his death, again and again, in whatever era and whatever place we may inhabit, for as long as there is a church."[7]

May it come to pass that abiding with him at this altar, we may receive sufficient grace to follow "in the blessed steps of his most holy life," and remain companions of Christ for all time to come.

8. ROMANS 5:1–17
"A BIBLE-CENTERED CHURCH?"

1

Everyone who walks into the sacred space of St. Thomas' Church [Hamilton, NY] faces an old-style stained glass window up front. It comes from a much earlier era in the Church when Morning Prayer was the main service on Sunday morning. This was an era when Bible reading and preaching were the general occupation of the service, when Holy Communion was celebrated once a month as well, perhaps, at an earlier service each week. The window is partially hidden by the reredos now in place behind the high altar. But its arrangement of classic icons is clearly visible: ancient symbols of the four New Testament Gospels surround a dove, a cross and a book.

The Holy Spirit [as a dove at the top] hovers over the cross. The cross, symbolizing the life of Christ, stands above the Bible to illuminate, to focus, and to suggest the truth of its ancient words. Something like a pictorial display of Martin Luther's observation that "the Bible is the cradle in which the Christ child is laid."

The book at the center stands for the Bible. On it is inscribed a rather threatening passage from the Book of the Prophet Isaiah [Isa 8:20]: "If they speak not according to this word, it is because there is no light in them." That warning is hard to read at a distance, but it declares that whoever is preaching from this pulpit better adhere to the teaching of the Bible.

2

This window makes me uncomfortable sometimes. For its arrangement of Christian symbols calls to mind an unpleasant incident at a diocesan clergy meeting several years ago. At that meeting I was publicly chastened by one of our young, very conservative priests.

We had gathered to have a conversation with the bishop about the future of the Church in this diocese. I had spoken in support of a more open and inclusive vision of the Christian community, and how we might begin to move in that direction. But I was quickly and sharply upbraided by this conservative young priest. He thought my words were somehow in conflict with what he called "the plain word of Scripture." He raised his voice, and in an unusual public gesture for a priest, shook his finger at me, and asked, "Don't you want a Bible-centered Church?" "No, indeed," I replied. "I want a Christ-centered Church!" It is the chalice, not a book however holy, that assures us of Christ's presence among us.

I reminded him that in most Episcopal churches, the altar is the central focus. It is here that we receive the very bread of heaven, and the cup of salvation. The lectern and the pulpit, with all their good and indispensable words, stand at the sides of the altar.

My challenging priest is no longer canonically resident in this Diocese. Others will have to worry about how best to relate to him. He may still be a problem. For his interchange with me was clear evidence that he has forgotten that Anglicans indeed take the Bible seriously, but not always literally.

3

We do take the Bible seriously, but honestly. We do this by reading the Bible in the light of the best scholarship available. By drawing on centuries of faithful interpretation. By seeing its ancient words building up the community of faith, empowering us to become a neighbor to the forgotten, and by bringing solace to the broken-hearted.

Dealing with the Bible is not an easy project, in part because it is really not one book, but a library of many books. The Old and New Testaments [39 and 27], together with the Apocrypha add up to 84 very different writings. Most modern editions can run to a thousand pages and more. We need all the help we can get with this anthology, so that we might stay with its life-forming treasures that are hidden between its covers, and separate its golden insights from its bad science and quite useless information.

For the biblical writings reflect the glories and the mistakes, the noble and ignoble attitudes, the beatific visions and the prejudices, the ideas, customs, achievements and failures of many people in many places, over many centuries. And even in the course of our three-year lectionary or cycle of readings, we read through only a fraction of the good parts.

We need some guidance to help us decide with what parts of the Bible we should aim to spend our time. We need some standard that will reveal the Bible's treasures, without distorting its basic message, or getting us bogged down in those parts that are of little religious use to us because their meaning is confined to the ancient times and ancient people who wrote them.

4

I want now to suggest very briefly a way of seeing how the Holy Spirit can point us to the life-giving Christ who is the chief subject of the Holy Scriptures. A way of honoring the Bible seriously but not literally in a Christ-centered Church.

This way simply emphasizes those biblical passages that already have found a warm place in our memories, that have brought comfort and support to us in happy and difficult times.

These are the words that remind us of God's unfailing promises, or hold before our consciousness the great vision of the better, the more just, the more humane life to which God calls us.

[1] Recall the covenant between Jacob and his father-in-law Laban: "May the Lord watch between me and thee while we are absent one from another." [Gen 32:40]

There are some occasions when those words might better inform our leave-taking than "So long," or "Have a nice day."

[2] Recall Ruth's moving plea to her mother-in-law Naomi:

"Entreat me not to leave you or to return from following you; for where you go, I will go, and where you lodge, I will lodge; your people shall be my people, and your God my God. Where you die, I will die; and there will I be buried." [Ruth 2:15–17]

Those words should shape what all lovers say to one another.

[3] You not have forgotten the Psalmist's poem of confidence:

"The Lord is my shepherd I shall not want. . . . He restores my soul. . . . Surely goodness and mercy shall follow me all the days of my life, and I shall dwell in the house of the Lord forever." [Ps 23]

How are we to face our death without those words?

[4] In the Nicene Creed we acknowledge that God speaks through the voice of the prophets. Their calls for fairness and charity are God's call to us. So recall the insistent plea of the prophet Amos:

"Let justice roll down like waters, and righteousness like an ever-flowing stream." [Amos 5:24]

Every move to compromise and to the delay of social healing stands indicted by those words.

[5] Think of Jesus' most open-ended invitation:

"Come unto me, all ye that travail and are heavy-laden, and I will give you rest" [Mth 22:28–29]

With these words, we know that it makes no difference who we are or where we have been.

[6] Jesus' words to the woman taken in adultery:

"Neither do I condemn you; go, and do not sin again." [Jn 8:22]

With those words in our mind, how can we be so quick to judge another?

[7] The picture of the Christian community that St. Paul recalls:

"There is no longer Jew or Greek. There is no longer slave or free. There is no longer male or female, for all of you are one in Christ Jesus." [Gal 3:18]

5

And to this list we surely will want to add one more—the opening announcement of today's Epistle reading: "We are justified by faith." [Rom 5:1] This is the summary proclamation of the Reformation: "The just shall live by faith." [Rom 1:17]

St. Paul's words clarify beyond all question what is most important of all: not commands, to be obeyed, however helpful. Not doctrines to be believed, however true. Not ceremonies to be performed, however uplifting. Not rules to be followed, however useful. But by the faithfulness and loyalty that count more than anything.

We will want to obey some commands, to believe some doctrines, to perform some ceremonies, to follow some rules. But we are "justified," brought into right relation with God and our neighbor by saying "yes" to the invitation to trust in God and to commit ourselves to doing justice where we live.

This is what it means to live well the life we have been loaned by God for a while.

Not displayed on windows, however sparkling. Not inscribed in a book, however sacred. But engraved on our heart and nourished by the self-offering of Christ at this most venerable altar.

9. MARK 10:2–16
"THE RIGHT THING TO DO"

1

Most people want to do the right thing. We count on others wanting to do that too. Doing this makes it possible for us to live together in our society, despite our different views on many matters. But deciding what the right thing is can sometimes be a difficult task.

Consider the Pharisees in today's Gospel [Mk 10:2–16]. They had it easy. They knew exactly where to look for the answer, and they certainly thought they knew the right question: "Is it lawful . . . ?" They asked. What does the rule-book say?

But Jesus' actions here and in many other places in the Gospels picture a very different approach and imply a different question.

Jesus put concern for persons over unquestioned adherence to rules. His way of deciding on the right thing to do upset the Pharisees, for they wanted clear, simple, yes-or-no answers, even to complex questions. Jesus' way puzzled his disciples as well. And it may make us uneasy at times. But the concern for human well-being was the clear a mark of Jesus' ministry and message. And that concern has become the defining mark of the company of women and men that came to take his name as their own.

In that law-obligated society of Jewish life in first century Palestine, the Pharisees' question seemed to be the right one: "Is it lawful . . ." But their approach missed the point of the Law altogether. If they had not been so concerned to trap Jesus, and if they had been more interested in the real-life situation of a problematic marriage, they would instead have asked, "What is the loving thing to do?" That seems to be the question Jesus has in mind.

2

Early on in St. Mark's Gospel [Mk 2] Jesus has shown how he approaches the crises in people's lives. His way is very different from that of the Pharisees.

Recall the story there of the paralyzed man who is brought to Jesus by some friends. The people have so crowded around Jesus that the paralytic's friends have to lower him down to Jesus through a hole they have cut in the roof. Jesus is impressed by their faith, forgives the paralytic his sins, heals his paralyzed body, and tells him to arise, take up his pallet and go on his way.

It is bad enough, said the Pharisees, that this man Jesus thought he could forgive sins. But he did this forgiving and healing on the Sabbath, when no work is to be done. He broke the Law.

Jesus did not ask "Is it permitted?" "Is it lawful . . . ?" Instead, he moves to respond to the disabling plight of a distressed human being. It is as if Jesus had asked of himself, "Now what is the loving, helpful thing to do?"

He then explained his action in a sentence that became a defining moment for the emerging community of Jesus' friends as they began to understand the boundless, the indiscriminately lavish nature of God's grace: "The Sabbath was made for humankind, not humankind for the Sabbath." [Mk 2:27–28] Or in the older more familiar King James Version, "The Sabbath was made for man, not man for the Sabbath." The commandments are not ends in themselves, but vehicles for the transformation, the support, the healing of all women and men.

Consider this: In the early years of the Second World War, the Nazi authorities were beginning to set in motion the death machinery of the Holocaust. The Gestapo came to a Catholic convent where a number of Jewish children had been hidden in the cloisters by the sisters. The Gestapo asked the Mother Superior, "Are there any Jews here?" "No, sir, there are not," she lied. The Gestapo officer surprisingly took her at her word and left. The children were sheltered there until the War was over. Although the Mother Superior had clearly told a material falsehood, in seeming violation of the commandment not to bear false witness, she had obeyed a higher law and saved human life.

St. Paul captured this new vision that Jesus is commending, and which the Mother Superior exemplified, when he says in his Letter to the Galatians, that ". . . the whole Law is fulfilled in one word: You shall love your neighbor as yourself." [Gal 5:14]

3

This same people-centered approach to discerning the right thing to do surfaces in Jesus' comments in today's Gospel about women and children. [Mk10:2–16]

In the Palestinian Jewish world of Jesus' day, a woman's situation was entirely determined by the important male in her life, whose property she was: father, husband, uncle. She had few choices. Her husband could divorce her easily, for whatever cause he chose, but no wife had that option. So Jesus' words about divorce and adultery, odd as they may seem, undercut all of that, and honor the personhood of the woman in a new and affirming way.

In the Palestinian Jewish world of Jesus' day, children were as vulnerable as women, equally subject to control by the father. And in the Roman cities where the gospel message would soon be proclaimed, infancy was even more perilous. For a Roman father could designate an infant for life or death.

But Jesus' words and actions about children undercut all of that, and honor the personhood of the child in a new and affirming way: "Let the little children come to me; forbid them not; for it is to such as these that the kingdom of God belongs."

Notice especially the words that Mark uses as he describes the situation of Jesus and the children: "touch," "took in his arms," "blessed," "laid hands on." These are "the official bodily actions of a father [in Roman law] designating a newly born infant for life rather than death, for accepting it into his family rather than casting it out . . .": touch, take in one's arms, bless, lay hands on.[8]

In the Kingdom that Jesus announces, accepting these "least ones" becomes the model for discipleship. And Christ's "kingdom people" are invited to become incarnations of Jesus' embrace and blessing of all the vulnerable ones in the world.

The Pharisees always asked, "Is it lawful?" But Jesus asked, "What does neighbor love call on me to do?"

In a *Time* essay, Andrew Sullivan wrote about the importance of stressing persons over rules:

". . . our religion, our moral life, is simply what we do. A Christian is not a Christian simply because she agrees to conform her life to some set of external principles or dogmas. . . . She is a Christian primarily because she acts like one. She loves and forgives; she listens and prays; she contemplates and befriends; her faith and her life fuse into an unself-conscious unity . . . practice is more important than theory, love is more important than law . . ."[9]

If Christ in his self-offering is our model, then we know that the loving thing is always the right thing to do.

10. MARK 9:30–37
"BEING FIRST AND LAST"

1

Jesus' disciples did not quite get it. Jesus claimed and tried to show that being on call for the wounded and suffering is the core of the faithful life to which

God calls us. The resurrection confirmed Jesus' belief and his live demonstration. But the disciples had a hard time understanding this.

Their lives had been transformed in their encounter with Jesus, almost like being moved from death to life. But they were still concerned with getting credit and a top place on some divine ledger. And this kept them from fully understanding the shattering change that Jesus was calling for.

I have always found it very curious that the inner circle of Jesus' disciples so misunderstood his mission and his message. They were so close, day after day, to him who was the face and agent of divine charity. But they still worried about gaining glory and having an honored position in the Kingdom of God that Jesus announced and embodied.

But, of course, believing is never easy, now or then. They experienced the world as we so often do: broken promises, unfeeling ingratitude, unanticipated deaths, the plain unfairness of things, and accidents, always accidents.

But it is in this very uncertain world where the good news of the providence of God makes it happen that we can share in Jesus' ministry of justice-making and compassion-sharing. We are, after all, not called to be flawless, but called to be faithful.

2

But back to the dense and befuddled disciples.

The very first thing Jesus did when he began his public ministry was to call some women and men to be his disciples. They traveled with him, learned from him, were inspired and nourished by him. They were the core of this new community of faith that one day would take his name as their own.

Their experience with Jesus convinced them that God was uniquely present and at work in his life. He had moved them from despair to new life, even as he does for us. He had brought release to those who had been captive to a demeaning style of life, even as he does for us. He had given them a sense of purpose, even as he does for us, and convinced them that God really does care.

But the old ways of thinking had a powerful hold on them. They still thought of "greatness" as a matter of rank and status. Recall how often Jesus had to remind them of another way. People always seemed surprised whenever he announced that in the Kingdom of God, the first will be last, and the last will be first. In the Kingdom of God all the world's usual priorities will be made topsy-turvy: "greatness" will mean service, not preferred seating; "greatness" will mean neighboring, not ranking; "greatness" will mean other-concern, not status-worry.

This picture Jesus was drawing was a direct challenge to the rabbinic tradition of his time that was so concerned about proper seating in the synagogue and at table, and for some, the proper seating order even in Paradise. Jesus would have none of this way of dividing people from one another. But the disciples had a hard time with his insistence on serving people rather than seeking a position of honor.

3

Consider some of the Gospel evidence.

At the Last Supper Jesus identifies the broken bread and the outpoured wine of the meal with his own body and blood soon to be broken and poured out in his impending death. He bids his friends, as often as they re-enact this action, to do it "for the remembrance" of him and his self-offering. But in the very next sentence we read that the disciples were discussing who among them was the greatest.

Three times in St. Mark's Gospel Jesus shares with the disciples his belief that he will soon suffer, be rejected by the chief priests, and be killed. And in the very next sentence, each time, we hear that the disciples were discussing who among them was the greatest.

They, who were so close to him, were still so very far from understanding his vision that the faithful life is being available to the other, no matter what the cost. But each time Jesus predicts his death, they worry about who is the greatest among them.

Now their confusion about "greatness" could reflect a concern about who would succeed to the leadership of their little apostolic community once Jesus is gone. That meaning shows up in *The Gospel of Thomas,* one of the dozen or so early gospels that were not included in the New Testament collection. There we read, "The disciples said to Jesus, 'We know that you will go away from us. Who is it that will then be great over us?'" [GThom 12] They were still thinking of "greatness" as "presiding" over others. But for Jesus "greatness" was to be "service." And his company of disciples will not need a powerful leader. It is to be a community of equals.

4

And so in today's Gospel [Mark 9:30–37] Jesus tries a different approach. Sensing that the disciples had been arguing among themselves once again about priorities of honor, he restates his conviction, and then demonstrates it:

"He said to them, 'Whoever wants to be first must be last of all and servant of all.' Then he took a little child and put it among them; and taking it in his arms, he said to them, 'Whoever welcomes one such child in my name welcomes me, and whoever welcomes me welcomes not me but the one who sent me.'"

Instead of *explaining* once more the life he was accepting for himself and enjoining on his followers, Jesus decided to *show* them. This was perhaps the most startling of all his great teaching moments.

He gathered up a child in his arms. Doing this was a dramatic way of showing that in the new community of faith being formed about him and that will do his work when he is gone, even the least important will be welcomed. Rank and honor and glory and privilege will count for nothing.

In that culture, a little child was indeed "to be last of all." But in the new society of Jesus' friends, this will all be turned around. Here hospitality will be shown to the most unlikely, the small, the powerless; here equal status will be given to all those who have none.

This should have been no surprise to those who had gathered about Jesus. Remember how often in the Gospel narratives Jesus is pictured as responding to the pleas of a parent on behalf of a sick or dying child.

When the disciples overcome the habits of their culture, and welcome such a child, they will be receiving him who came not to be served, but to serve, and to give his life as a ransom for many.

This is the life which Jesus exemplifies. This is the life to which he invites us all. This is the blessed life which our baptism in his name has enjoined upon us all. This is the life in which we have been marked as Christ's own forever.

11. EPHESIANS 6:10–20
"PUT ON THE WHOLE ARMOR OF GOD"

1

I was born and grew up in Goshen, Indiana, the county seat of Elkhart County, right in the middle of the border with the State of Michigan. This is an area with very substantial Amish, Brethren, and Mennonite populations. They are the modern-day heirs of the Anabaptist wing of the 16th century Protestant Reformation.

The Anabaptists were persecuted by both the Roman Catholic and mainstream Protestant churches, including, alas, our own Anglican forbears. But they survived, and their special view of the Gospel continues to be a powerful model for many people who take seriously the New Testament call to live a holy life. We may not share many of their views, but we can surely learn from their effort to live by their understanding of the Gospel, often at great personal cost.

They got their name in this way: At the beginning, most of them had been baptized as infants in the Roman Catholic or one of the major Protestant Churches. But they regarded this as no baptism at all. They insisted that baptism was only for adults. They called it "believer's baptism." And so when they joined one of these new congregations, they were baptized again, and thus came to be called "re-baptizers" or "Anabaptists."

They regarded Baptism and the Eucharist as "ordinances" but not grace-conveying sacraments. They practiced foot-washing twice or more a year, in a way that involved the whole congregation. They insisted on the separation of church and state—an unthinkable novelty in the 16th century. For many years some did not use musical instruments in worship. And no matter what the situation, they steadfastly refused military service. No Christian, they said, has a *jus gladii*, "the right of the sword." Along with the Church of the Brethren, and the Friends [or Quakers], they became known in this country as the "Peace Churches."

They had two special concerns. One was to undo the fifteen centuries of developing doctrine and liturgy that Anglicans so prize. They did this in order to return to what they regarded as the simple, original, first-century form of Christian life. Their second concern was to have as little to do as possible with the habits and values of the world.

I grew up and went to school with friends from these churches. Their family names were seldom heard in upstate New York until recently, when some Mennonite families settled in nearby Madison: Smucker, Hostetler, Graber, Hershberger, Brunk, Stoltzfus, Swartzendruber, Umble, Yoder, and Wenger. On the very day in April, 1943 when I enlisted in the United States Army, some of those childhood friends began the process to be recognized and registered as Conscientious Objectors. For them, this meant substituting a life in community service camps for duty in the nation's war camps.

I no longer have any family ties that draw me back to Goshen any more. And so it has been a sentimental experience for me, of late, to see a Mennonite booth at the Farmers' Market, recognizably Mennonite shoppers at the Grand Union, and an occasional horse and buggy on the highway, supported by signs the Department of Transportation has put up at strategic spots, asking us to a "share the road." Perhaps Hamilton might someday have what still is heavily used in Goshen, a parking lot with a sign that says "For Horse-drawn Vehicles Only."

2

Now all of this may seem a bit quaint or irrelevant to many, perhaps most of you, and a strange thing to do in a sermon. But my reciting it is motivated, in part, by trying to call attention, in a very round-about way, to St. Paul's cautionary words in his Letter to the Ephesians [Eph 6:10–20], to "put on the whole armor of God." Despite its obviously military language, this passage from Ephesians was very important to the peace-motivated Mennonites and Brethren that I knew now so long ago. And to their ancestors at the time of the Reformation as well.

St. Paul was convinced that there are strong forces in the world that really do oppose the Christian vision. He was convinced that there are powers and structures in the world that make living the Christian life a difficult and perilous enterprise. The struggle against their influence and domination is a serious and on-going effort. The Anabaptists, then and now, knew that to be true from personal experience.

And so these radical Protestants separated themselves as much as they could from the offices and policies and assumptions of the world. But their idea of "shunning the world" had a positive corollary, then as now. The Anabaptist vision was to serve the world: reject its sub-Christian preferences and practices, but serve its human needs; witness to the way of peace, and transform what can be saved.

They rejected what the world favors, but committed themselves, then and now, to do the healing work of the Gospel: to reduce hostility, to tend to the victims, to replace hate with compassion. In our own time, Mennonite relief agencies challenge the priorities of the world in many places, and in many ways. They seek to enable life where the powers of the world work for death. They have had a long-standing service and relief presence in Palestine, for example.

3

St. Paul implores us "to put on the whole armor of God," and in this way to resist and "stand firm" against everything that opposes Christ's call to a saving and servant life.

He uses ancient military language, and then turns the whole fighting enterprise upside down: belt, breastplate, shoes, shield, helmet, and sword. These are all the things a Roman soldier would need to do battle against his enemies in the empire of death and slavery.

But notice what the Gospel costume is. The theologian Walter Wink calls it "spiritual weaponry"—truth, righteousness, peace, faith, salvation, the Spirit.[10]

"Armor of God," "spiritual weaponry"—strange, almost contradictory terms. But linking "armor" and "God," or "spiritual" and "weaponry" has the bold effect of stressing just how difficult it can be to live a life of Christian obedience in a culture that entices us with so many alluring but inimical interests.

To talk about the "armor of God" or "spiritual weaponry" highlights rhetorically just how serious the conflict is between the Gospel call for charity and compassion, and the world's desire for domination. To talk about the "armor of God" or "spiritual weaponry" highlights rhetorically just how serious the conflict is between the Gospel call for sharing and the world's wont for possession; just how serious the conflict is between the Gospel sanction for sacrifice and the world's endorsement of greed.

St. Paul calls these foes of faith by rather strange names, drawn from the pre-scientific mythology of the age. We fight, he said, "against the cosmic powers of this present darkness, against the spiritual forces of evil in the heavenly places." [Eph 6:12]

But what makes the Christian life harder than we had thought is not something supernatural or mythological, but attitudes we have learned from the world, attitudes that are quite natural—and all the more subverting to faith.

In the Litany for Ash Wednesday, the Prayer Book names some of these worldly ways, some of these demonic attitudes and actions that so easily insinuate themselves into our lives. Against them we need all the "spiritual weaponry" we can find:

"Our self-indulgent appetites and ways, . . . our blindness to human need and suffering, our indifference to injustice and cruelty; . . . uncharitable thoughts toward our neighbors, our prejudice and contempt toward those who differ from us; our waste and pollution of [God's] creation, and our lack of concern for those who come after us . . ." [PB, 267–269]

Only "the armor of God" can protect us from their attacks, and give us time and space to purge their venom from our souls. It is almost enough to warrant bringing back into occasional parish use one of my least favorite hymns: "Onward, Christian Soldiers"

> "Onward, Christian soldiers, marching as to war,
> With the cross of Jesus going on before."[11]

4

St. John's Gospel [Jn 6:56–69] illustrates in story form this opposition of the satisfactions of the world and the unprecedented contributions of Christ. An opposition the Anabaptists perceived and St. Paul described.

Once again Jesus has identified his self-offering as the Bread from Heaven that gives eternal life. Many people in his audience found this declaration so different from anything they expected, so opposed to the ordinary sense of things, so much in conflict with the notions of the world that they gave up trying to think in this new way Jesus authorized. They finally admitted, "This is not for us." And they abandoned Jesus in one of the saddest lines in the New Testament:

"Because of this many of his disciples turned back and no longer went about with him." [Jn 6:66]

But those who stayed, then and now, received the "bread that never runs out, bread that satisfies forever, bread that is always enough."

12. II CORINTHIANS 12:2–10
"MY GRACE IS SUFFICIENT FOR THEE"

1

Not long after the death of Jesus, groups of believers, encouraged and empowered by the lively presence among them of the Risen Jesus, began to meet in one another's homes, for what they called "the breaking of the bread and the prayers"—that is, for the Holy Eucharist.

Not just in Jerusalem and the villages of Palestine, but before long in some of the large cities scattered around the Mediterranean world of the Roman Empire—Ephesus, Philippi, Corinth, Thessalonica, and even Rome.

But how did these Christian house assemblies in such widely separated places ever become the "one holy catholic and apostolic church"? There was no internet, no radio, no email, no electronic communication. How was it that they did not each go their separate ways? How was it that they seemed to think of themselves as belonging to the same developing movement of faith and hospitality, as belonging to the one Body of Christ?

They did not have the internet, but they had St. Paul.

He had helped to organize some of these congregations. Others had different beginnings. But with all of them, Paul felt the need to keep in close, personal touch. And writing letters [or epistles] was his way of doing just that.

He encouraged these young churches to pass his letters around, to share them with one another: "And when this letter has been read among you, have it read also in the church of the Laodiceans; and see that you read also the letter from Laodicea." [Col. 4:16]

In this way his letters symbolized and helped to effect the unity that these colonies of believing women and men came to have with one another.

2

St. Paul regarded his letters as substitutes for his personal presence. Just as our letters to friends and family substitute for our being right there with those whom we love.

But his letters tell us something more. They let us in on the new language that St. Paul was developing to help these new Christian church gatherings talk about their faith—a way of believing that took its cue from the person and teachings and lived example of Jesus of Nazareth.

St. Paul's suggestions have continued to be mottos for our own religious life. Let me remind you of just some of them. For these phrases and sentences from his letters have etched themselves deeply into the consciousness of faithful women and men across the centuries and over the continents.

[1] Sometimes St. Paul says clearly what makes the Christian life possible, and how the norms and values of the world must not define the community of faith.

"The one who is righteous will live by faith." [Rom 1:17]

"Do not be conformed to this world, but be transformed by the renewing of your mind."

"Let the same mind be in you that was in Christ Jesus." [Phil 2:5]

[2] Sometimes St. Paul reminds us that in the Church private interest must give way to a concern for the common good.

"In church I would rather speak five words with my mind in order to instruct others, than ten thousand words in a tongue." [I Cor 14:19]

"Brothers and sisters, do not be weary in well-doing, in doing what is right." [II Thess 3:13]

"Be subject to one another out of reverence for Christ." [Eph 5:21]

[3] Sometimes St. Paul tries to show that doing what God commands can only mean doing the works of love.

"Love does no wrong to a neighbor; therefore, love is the fulfilling of the Law." [Rom 13:10]

"Faith, hope, and love abide, these three; and the greatest of these is love."[I Cor 13:13]

"We walk by faith not by sight." [I ICor 5:7]

"We have this treasure in earthen vessels, so that it may be made clear that this extraordinary power belongs to God, and does not come from us." [II Cor 4:7]

"Rejoice always; pray without ceasing." [I Thess 5:17]

[4] Sometimes St. Paul reminds us that in the Church the worldly distinctions of social situation, economic status, or gender identity have no relevance.

"From now on, we regard no one from a human point of view." [II Cor 5:16]

"There are varieties of gifts, but the same Spirit . . . To each is given the manifestation of the Spirit for the common good" [I Cor 12:4, 7]

"There is no longer Jew or Greek, there is no longer slave or free, there is no longer male and female, for all of you are one in Christ Jesus'" [Gal 3:28]

It is hard to imagine how we might begin to talk about our hopes, about our gratitude, about our beliefs without using some of the words of St. Paul. He has given lasting form to the vocabulary of our faith.

3

And to this list we must surely add the verse from today's Epistle [II Cor 12:2–10]—"My grace is sufficient for you." This is one more of these lines in which St. Paul sums up in so very few words the heart and substance of the attitude toward life that Christian faith makes possible: "My grace is sufficient for you.", ["My grace is sufficient for thee." KJV]

The grace of which St. Paul speaks, of course, is not his, but the grace of Christ.

St. Paul tells us that there was something in his own personal life which he found almost too much to bear. He called it a "thorn in the flesh." But we do not know what this problem was: epilepsy, malaria, glaucoma, sexual temptation? Whatever it was, it plagued him throughout his life. He prayed for deliverance from it, but to no avail.

But the response he did get was the assurance that the grace of God was more than adequate to enable him to live with the problem even if there were no cure.

The "thorn in the flesh" remained, but in the power of God's grace, that problem, whatever it was, could not immobilize him, nor dampen the ardor of his faith, nor chill his enthusiasm for the Gospel. He took seriously to heart Jesus' counsel: "My grace is sufficient for you."

From time to time, some of the other heavy lines from St. Paul's letters may come to save us. But if not, perhaps we will look back on all the ways in which God's compassion continuingly restores our life, and makes it possible for us to endure to the end with grace and peace. And then we will know in our own lives for sure, the truth of Jesus' response to St. Paul in his dilemma: "My grace is sufficient for you."

13. JOHN 15:9–17
"ON BEING COMMANDED TO LOVE"

1

One of my most treasured memories is reading to our daughters—Martha and Ruth—when they were very young. One of our favorite authors was Joan Walsh Anglund. The titles of her books read like a children's library:

A Friend Is Someone Who Likes You
Spring Is a New Beginning
Christmas Is a Time of Giving

And her best and the one we read most often: *Love Is a Special Way of Feeling.*

The titles are so true. They help us speak of very complex realities to the very young in a simple way, easy to understand. In each case, of course, something more needs to be said. What the little book titles say about friendship, Spring, Christmas, and love is really true. Whatever else friends are, they are those people who unbelievably like us. Spring really is the time when many things begin again. Christmas really does move us to be givers. And when one loves, one feels a very special way about the other. But in each case, the truth of the titles is partial. There is something more than needs to be said.

That is especially so with the last book. Love is indeed a "special way of feeling," but if that is all it is, the Christian Gospel makes no sense. If love is only a "special way of feeling," then Jesus' directive in today's Gospel [Jn 15:9–17] will fall on deaf ears: "This is my commandment that you love one another."

We have known from the beginning that love is at the very heart of the Christian vision of the forgiven and forgiving life. But how can we be *commanded* to love?

Someone might suggest, recommend, invite, implore, hope, encourage, or beseech us to love. But our feelings cannot be summoned up by a command from Jesus, from ourselves, or from anyone else. We cannot become loving persons just because someone has told us to be.

2

We have a clue to what the injunction in the Gospel is really all about when we turn to the Epistle reading [I Jn 4:7–21]. The Epistle readings for three successive weeks have been drawn from the First Letter of John, and we have already been reminded that "we are God's children *now*." [I Jn 3:2]

Not later, when we believe enough. Not later, when we have done enough. Not later, when we have worked hard enough. Not later, when we have waited long enough. But "we are God's children *now*."

If we are *now* already God's children, we ought *now* to begin looking at one another in this new way. The loving way is first of all a new way of regarding one another.

St. John has reminded us that we are ". . . not to love in word or speech; but in truth and action." [I Jn 3:18]

St. John asks us to see that love is not just a new way of looking or feeling, as important as that is. It is to be a new way of acting.

Love is not just a new way of regarding one another. We are able now and expected now to do something more than just regard one another differently.

3

And now in the Epistle St. John makes quite clear what sort of love is at the heart of the Christian life. This can help us understand just what Jesus had in mind by commanding it of us.

In the first place, and with absolutely no surprise, it has to do with an injunction to *act* lovingly toward our neighbor, not just to *feel* lovingly.

And actions rather than feelings can be commanded. To love in the Christian way requires, then, that we do the loving thing, even if we do not feel very loving. To love in the Christian way means that we do whatever it is that love needs to have done, no matter how we may feel.

Obeying Jesus' command would be an impossible burden if we had to depend on our own power, on our own talent, on our own skill or insight.

But hear again St. John's moving affirmation of what makes the Gospel way of life a real possibility: "We love because he first loved us."

That simple declaration frees us forever from the panic of trying to summon up enough strength on our own to do the loving thing. Clearly impossible.

That simple declaration frees us forever to live a grateful life that accepts joyfully the divine generosity.

That simple declaration enables us to embrace the largesse of God that comes before all else, that surrounds us and supports us all the day long.

That simple declaration frees Jesus' word from being a heavy, impossible command, and transforms it into a liberating, divine permission.

Many years ago theologians used to call this "prevenient grace." A strange-sounding term for a very simple truth. "Prevenient grace" was simply a technical way to express what Christian women and men, young and old, have always known:

That we have been brought into life by another. That we are continually surrounded by a great love who nurtures and sustains us, and who makes it happen that now and then we are able to do what love requires us to do, for those with whom God has placed us together in this life.

So let St. John's words be written on our hearts and graven on our minds. Then the faithful will know that the command to love is no heavy burden. It is God's great gift.

St. John's words give permission to what otherwise would be an impossible demand:

"We love because he first loved us."

14. MARK 4:41
"THEY FEARED A GREAT FEAR"

1

Early in the week the very Protestant pastor will ask, "What should I preach about next Sunday?" He or she then tries to find an answer to that sometimes vexing question: Reflecting on favorite Bible verses, wondering if there is something going on in the local church that needs some attention, relives or awakens some personal interests, enlivens some good ideas,

The pastor's question is not a surprise, since the sermon is the main focus of a Protestant service. So much so that John Calvin, one of the most influential voices of the Protestant Reformation, said that "to go to Church" was really "to go to the sermon."

Not so—for one who preaches in the Anglican tradition. Unless the service is Morning Prayer with its own integrity, the sermon is normally followed by a celebration of the Holy Eucharist. Here the service is twofold: the Word is spoken and then the divine Word of remission and grace is acted out. By the breaking of the bread and pouring out of the wine. And that makes all the difference,

An Anglican priest does not ask early in the week, "What should I preach about next Sunday?" Instead, the question is "What word, what image, what claim or what picture in the Collect or the Lessons appointed in the Prayer Book weighs on my heart or mind today? What in these texts constrains my attention at this moment"?

An Anglican priest does not begin with private interests, but with the biblical freight of the appointed readings. Where in the Psalm, the Old Testament passage, or the Epistle reading, where in the Gospel is the word of grace, the word of "redemption and release" that needs to be lifted up and reflected on today? Where in these pages is the Gospel promise of compassion? Where is the word of recovery that needs to be heard today? How might we be reminded today of the Gospel assurance of the unfailing presence alongside us of him who wipes the slate clean, who makes new beginnings always possible?

The priest surely knows that at every celebration of the Holy Eucharist there will be someone who truly needs to hold anew God's precious gift of absolution. That at every celebration there will be someone who truly needs and wills to take to heart once again the assurance that God does indeed forgive our sin.

The priest will never know and needs never to know, whether the spoken words at the pulpit or the acted out words at the altar will be more saving, more life-giving, and more up-building for the common good of those who believe.

But the priest is nourished and upheld by the promise that if the pulpit words fail to renew, the altar deeds will unfailingly remedy the loss.

2

Still, crafting a sermon for the Prayer Book service is an assignment of special importance. Its preparation for an Anglicans priest must always begin by putting aside personal preferences and instead giving careful attention to the Lessons appointed for that day.

I have always tried to do just that. I usually read the lectionary readings several times over the course of a day or two. At this point in my life, I find that the assigned readings are really quite familiar, and much of my Colgate teaching career focused on the New Testament Gospels. You would think there would be no surprises when sermon preparation begins. But that is not always the case. The words may indeed be familiar, about their power may become very new, and their ability to change one's attention may be very new.

I recall when I was last reflecting on the Lessons for Holy Week. I was reading St. Luke's account of Jesus' painful encounter with the Jerusalem authorities opposed to him and his ministry. [Lk 23:6–12] St. Luke describes Jesus interview with Pilate, the Roman procurator or governor. He could find no fault with Jesus. But the chief priests and the crowd were not satisfied with that view. So Pilate sent Jesus to Herod who had jurisdiction in Galilee, and

Jesus was after all a Galilean. After an unsatisfactory interview, Herod sent Jesus back to Pilate. Then St. Luke adds this explanatory comment:

"That same day Herod and Pilate became friends with each other; before this they had been enemies." [Lk 23:12]

The words may be familiar, but how they weigh upon the sermon preparer and the congregation may be very new. St. Luke's comment about the new friendship of Pilate and Herod reminded me afresh of how the religious and political powers of Jesus' day conspired to do him in. [If one reads the Lessons carefully, there is always the possibility of being surprised.]

3

Finding something a bit hidden in today's Lessons was a similar experience, but it came about in a different way. Instead of puzzling over the few paragraphs assigned for today, I once again at one sitting, read over the whole of St. Mark's Gospel. I rediscovered in that way the quite startling effect Jesus had on those who encountered him, or who worked with him.

Today's Gospel is St. Mark's short narrative of Jesus stilling a storm on the Sea of Galilee. And what was the disciples' response? "They were filled with great awe . . ." [Mk 4:41]

A literal, word-for-word translation of the Greek text would say of the disciples: "They feared a great fear."

Now that may be acceptable Greek, but it is not very good English. So translators have suggested several other possibilities: The disciples were "awestruck, startled, amazed, stunned, astonished, full of wonder, surprised, utterly amazed, in awe, they feared exceedingly." All these are better English than the literal Greek: "they feared a great fear."

And what I saw once again by reading the complete Gospel at one sitting was how often the disciples responded in just that way to their encounter with Jesus—surprise, amazement, astonishment, and over and over again, "they feared with a great fear."

Over and over again in St. Mark's Gospel, when they heard what he said, when they saw what he was doing, when they began to sense who he was— "they feared a great fear."

Who else had ever said, "Whoever does the will of God is my brother and my sister and mother." [Mk 3:31–35]

Who else had ever healed a paralytic let down at his feet, saying, ". . . take up your mat and go to your home . . . They were all amazed, and glorified God, saying 'We have never seen anything like this.'" [Mk 2:1–12]

Who else had ever still a storm at sea, got into the boat with his friends, and the wind ceased. "And they were utterly astounded." [Mk 6:44–52]

We should not be surprised that they "feared a great fear."

4

And all of this is with great welcome confirmed by the Epistle reading for today, written perhaps twenty years before St. Mark's Gospel was circulating among the Christian assemblies. St. Paul announces and explains just why it was that Jesus' followers and friends were so surprised by what he said, by what he did, and indeed, by who he was. St. Paul announces and explains just what this new life is like that Jesus makes possible, and which he has enjoined upon us: "From now on," he wrote, "we regard no one from a human point of view." [II Cor 5:16]

In our new life in Christ the distinctions of the world have become irrelevant. In the Body of Christ no one can be judged on the basis of external standards—economic status, social role, or gender identity. For by our baptism we are made a new creation.

The human point of view that rules the unbelieving world has been replaced by the point of view of Christ that constrains us, that obliges, compels, and lays a claim on us. As St. Paul wrote to the Christians in Rome, we are not to be conformed to the world, with its standards of worth and importance, but to be transformed by the power of God's unsolicited grace. [Rom 12:1]

In the new life of faith, we are transformed by the blessing of Christ on us, who beckons us always to respect the otherness of the other—in nurture and presence, in sympathy and regard, in comfort and compassion.

That we should be allowed and gifted with such a joyous presence is amazement and surprise enough for a lifetime. We may not "fear a great fear," but we will be astonished and unaccountably pleased with our new life in Christ. And so might those others whom we meet on our way.

For in this new life to which we are called—"The poor receive help, the sinner is given understanding and help, the hungry are fed, the sick are healed, and the enemy is loved."[12]

Or as Elie Wiesel, the Nobel Laureate and Holocaust survivor said in a recent Commencement address, "There must be on this planet one person who needs you. Do not turn away."[13]

15. MATTHEW 25:15–22
"GIVE TO CAESAR..."

1

Most of us have never lived under enemy occupation. Others have, of course: Native Americans beginning with the European colonization; Blacks in South Africa during Apartheid; Palestinians since 1948. All of these knew what it means to live under the authority of some other power. And so did Jesus, and all his contemporaries.

People who are being subjugated tend to close ranks, to downplay or to set aside their differences, and to present a common front in the face of the enemy, with occasional uprisings and protests. For so long as there is occupation, there will be resistance.

But Jesus seemed to have had no interest in joining demonstrations or rebellions against the garrisons of the Roman army occupying Palestine. And that may help to account for some of the opposition that he encountered among his own people.

Jesus was more concerned with denouncing religious hypocrisy wherever he saw it, than protesting against the power of Rome. And this may help us answer a question that lurks beneath the texts of the New Testament Gospels.

The question is this: What could Jesus possibly have done or said that was so serious as to have persuaded some of his fellow religious Jews to accuse him of being unpatriotic? What could Jesus possibly have done or said that was so serious as to have persuaded some of his fellow religious Jews to look for some pretext to turn him over to the detested Roman authorities for execution?

Under Roman occupation the small religious party of Pharisees was convinced that the survival of Jewish identity required complete conformity to the Torah or Law of Moses. But the Gospels tell us that Jesus was rather relaxed about such things as Sabbath observance.

He socialized with religiously improper persons. He suggested that the "People of God" are not defined by family ties, by purity codes, or by ethnic considerations. He talked and acted as if meeting another's need is always more important than following social convention, or even obeying the Law of Moses.

Such attitudes and actions made it almost inevitable that Jesus would encounter opposition, provoke critics, and make powerful enemies among his own people, almost from the beginning of his ministry.

2

And so the most clever of Jesus' critics looked or arranged for ways in which they could entrap him into doing or saying something publicly subversive of their religious tradition, or sufficiently anti-Roman as to arouse the interest and intervention of the occupying authorities.

This is the very situation we meet in the reading for today from the Gospel according to Matthew [Mth25:15–22] Biblical scholars call this kind of narrative an "entrapment story." And there are others like it in the New Testament.

St. John's Gospel has a story that is very similar to today's Gospel.[Jn 8:1–11] In this story some men bring before Jesus a woman caught in an act of adultery. [The man involved, of course, got away and is not part of the story.] They aim to entrap Jesus, to put him on the spot. If Jesus forbids them to stone her to death, then he would be violating the clear demand of the Law of Moses. That would show that Jesus was not much interested in preserving Jewish identity, so threatened as it was under Roman occupation.

But if he allows them to stone her, then he would be inviting the antagonism and intervention of the Roman authorities, for they reserved capital punishment for themselves.

Jesus avoided their trap, and made it clear that responding to the woman's desperate need was of first importance to him. So he said to her accusers who had sought to trap him, "Let him who is without sin among you cast the first stone." And to the woman he said, in perhaps the most generous word in the entire Bible, "I do not condemn you. Go your way, and do not sin again."

His critics were amazed, and went away. Not because Jesus was so clever as to avoid their trap. But because Jesus saw through their hypocrisy. And for Jesus that was most serious, since he found hypocrisy to be the "source sin" of so much unfaithfulness.

For fidelity to God cannot be defined by obeying the letter of the Law, even then Law of Moses.

Nor can it be measured by quantities of gifts—since all that we are and all that we have we have received from God.

Fidelity to God is shown by sharing with others the compassion that God showers on our lives.

Jesus' critics were well to be amazed. For the only fitting response to Jesus is a great amazement—the surprise that as unlovable as we can be, we have been loved by a most generous love, nevertheless.

Jesus' critics were well to be amazed. For the only fitting response to Jesus is a great astonishment—the surprise that dead-ended as our lives might seem to be, we have been graced by the gospel of another chance, nevertheless.

3

There is another early Christian text that may help us see the point of Jesus' response to those who sought to entrap him in the discussion of Caesar's image on the coin.

Matthew, Mark, Luke, and John were not the only Gospels to have been written. In the decades after Jesus' death, there were perhaps a dozen other Gospels circulating at various times and in various communities of Christians. Full or partial texts of most of these "other Gospels" have been found and studied.

One of these is *The Gospel of Thomas*. This Gospel does not tell us much about Jesus' life, but it does transmit some of his words and teachings. It includes a version of St. Matthew's story that we heard today—the story of the Pharisees' attempt to entrap Jesus with the question about paying taxes to Caesar.

Here, as in St. Matthew's version, Jesus says, "Give to Caesar what belongs to Caesar. Give to God what belongs to God."

But in Thomas' version, Jesus adds another line: "And give to me what belongs to me." [GThomLog. 100]

"Give to me what belongs to me." That, I think, is the real meaning of the story.

Jesus' critics were amazed and went away.

We too are amazed. But we will stay to give to Jesus what belongs to him. We will stay to learn from him and to pray.

Jesus' critics were amazed and went away. But we will stay to give thanks for the unimaginable surprise of grace.

And in doing this, we will give to Christ what belongs to him, as he asks us to do.

16. MARK 8:27–38
QUESTIONS THE BIBLE ASKS

1

When bad things happen, we turn to family and friends for counsel and company. The blessed ones will find support in the community of faith, and its great gifts of memory and patience.

Many will find themselves nourished by the Holy Eucharist. Others will be sustained by the treasures of grace that our tradition conveys.

Some of these considerable gifts are given to us in the three books that have helped to shape how we worship in the Anglican way: the Prayer Book, the Hymnal, and the Bible. Each of these books brings a special merit to ease our distress.

When bad things happen, *The Prayer Book* will help us to pray: "And we most humbly beseech thee, of thy goodness, O Lord, to comfort and succor all those who, in this transitory life, are in trouble, sorrow, need, sickness, or any other adversity." [BCP 329]

Or this: "But thou art the same Lord whose property is always to have mercy. [BCP 337]

When bad things happen, *The Hymnal* will help us to sing: "Amazing grace, how sweet the sound . . ." [671]

Or this: "God moves in a mysterious way, his wonders to perform." [677]

Or this: "Were the whole realm of nature mine, that were an offering far too small; love so amazing, so divine, demands my soul, my life, my all." [474]

When bad things happen, *The Bible* will assure us that the merciful shall receive mercy, that the meek will inherit the earth, that peacemakers shall be called the children of God. [Mth 5:1–11], and that in God's remarkable house there are indeed many mansions, where we have been promised a place. [Jn 14:2]

And so, if we have favorite prayers, favorite hymns, and favorite passages of Scripture we will never be alone or lost when bad things happen.

2

But we find something else when we turn to the Bible, in good times or bad. Scattered here and there in the Bible are some *questions* that need to be reckoned with, not just answers to be relied on. There are questions to be worried about, not just assurances to give us comfort. The Bible does not give us simply promises to sustain us, but sometimes it gives puzzles and cautions to give us pause.

[a] Consider the sorry tale of the two brothers in the first Genesis family. Cain is angry that God prefers the offering of Abel, his shepherd brother, to his own offering from the harvest. In his jealous rage, Cain kills Abel. But God suspects that something is amiss, and so says to Cain, "Where is your brother, Abel?"

Cain's response to this divine inquiry is a question that haunts every person of faith who wonders sometimes just how much of themselves they can give in concern and care for another: "And Cain said, 'Am I my brother's keeper?'" [Gen.4:9]

For us ever to be tempted to ask that question is to admit just how far we have moved from sharing the life that is the divine intent for the human family. "Am I my brother's keeper?" That will always be one of the Bible's most troubling questions.

[b] Consider the astonishment of the Psalmist. This poet realizes that the nourishing power of God surrounds and upholds us always, everywhere, no matter what despite we do to the divine grace. And so his question turns into a grateful sigh of relief: "Where can I go from your spirit [O God]? Or where can I flee from your presence?" [Ps 139:7]

The answer to which he comes is the inner meaning of the acclamation in the ancient Creed of Nicea which we will soon say together "We believe in one God . . . maker of heaven and earth, of all that is, seen and unseen.

The psychologist Carl Jung shared this Psalmist's conviction, and had on a plaque over his front door and inscribed on his tombstone: "Bidden or not bidden, God is present." [*Vocatus atque non vocatus deus aderit."*]

The same Psalmist who asked the question phrases an answer in an even more poetic way: "If I take the wings of the morning, and dwell in the farthest limits of the sea, even there your hand shall lead me, and your right hand shall hold me fast." [Ps 139:9, 10]

[c] Consider the prophet Micah's final question. He has made his way through the 613 commandments enjoined by the "Law of Moses". And now he has discovered that the truly religious life worries much more about care for persons than following rules.

Micah's question frames in the simplest way the serious question of all who seek to attend to the divine imperative and hope for human life: "What does the Lord require of you?" he asked. [Micah 6:8]

His *question* challenges all those who pursue complicated programs for preservation or change: "What does the Lord require of you?"

The *answer* to which he comes helps us to pierce through the fog of all these competing claims of what we, who believe and seek to serve, ought to do:

"He has shown you . . . what is good. And what does the Lord require of you, but to do justice, to love kindness, and to walk humbly with God."

3

Consider at last the question Jesus puts to his disciples, then and now, in the Gospel appointed for today: "But who do you say that I am?" [Mk 8:29//s]

Jesus is now about to leave his home area in northern Palestine, and take his reforming mission to Jerusalem, the religious and political center of the Jewish world.

He seems to be concerned about how people are regarding his mission and ministry. And so he asks his disciples traveling with him, "What do you hear about me? What are people saying?" Their report was not surprising: "Everybody seems to think you are some sort of a prophet, somebody doing God's work for this broken world."

"But you have been closer to me than anybody else. Who do you say that I am?" Jesus asked. "You are the Christ, the Messiah," blurts out Peter, "an agent of God's call to forgive and to share." "Don't tell anyone," says Jesus, "for people will get the wrong idea and expect me to lead guerilla attacks on the garrisons of the Roman army occupying Palestine.

"But I'm going to be a different kind of Messiah. Not a king, but a servant. Not a dominating leader, but a brother who will stand in solidarity with those who suffer in any way. Not working to get others to pay attention to me, but working to let everybody know what God is willing to do, and how far God is willing to go to remedy their need."

But this is not what Peter had in mind. He was not worrying so much about Jesus being a servant Messiah, but was worrying about himself. For he had a hunch that Jesus might expect his disciples to lead a servant life too. Instead of a pursuit of glory, the self-offering of Jesus is going to be the pattern for all.

Jesus asks, "But who do you say that I am?" And we will soon answer his question in the fourth century words of the Nicene Creed:

> ". . . God from God, Light from Light,
> true God from true God,
> begotten, not made,
> of one Being with the Father . . ."

But having the right words is not enough. Peter had that. We more fully answer Jesus' question by the way we live with one another in the world. As St. Peter will soon learn, to acknowledge Jesus to be the Christ is to commit oneself to a life policy of caring and being for one another, no matter what.

If there is any doubt about this, Jesus puts it to rest with his final question to his disciples, then and now. To repeat it and to ask it of ourselves means we already know the answer: "But what shall it profit someone to gain the whole world, and lose their own soul?" [Mk 8:36]

NOTES

1. Barbara Brown Taylor, *Christian Century*, July 25, 2006.

2. "Come together in common, one and all without exception, in charity, in one faith and in one Jesus Christ, who is of the race of David according to the flesh, the Son of Man and the Son of God, so that with undivided mind you may obey the bishops and the priests, and break one Bread which is the medicine of immortality, and the antidote against death, enabling us to live forever in Jesus Christ." {St. Ignatius of Antioch, 110 AD]

3. Blessed Lord, who caused all holy Scriptures to be written for our learning; Grant us so to hear them, read, mark, learn, and inwardly digest them, that we may embrace and ever hold fast the blessed hope of everlasting life, which you have given us in our Savior Jesus Christ; who lives and reigns with you and the Holy Spirit, one God, for ever and ever. Amen.

4.. Blessed Lord, who caused all holy Scriptures to be written for our learning; Grant us so to hear them, read, mark, learn, and inwardly digest them, that we may embrace and ever hold fast the blessed hope of everlasting life, which you have given us in our Savior Jesus Christ; who lives and reigns with you and the Holy Spirit, one God, for ever and ever. Amen.

5. See Roger Ferlo, *Sensing God [Reading With All Our Senses],* Cambridge, MA: Cowley Publications, 2002.

6. "The substitution of doves and lambs in Temple worship comes as a relief," and a happy substitute for human sacrifice, "but it is important to remember that the Temple in which Jesus walked was soaked in blood." [Barbara Cawthorne Crafton, "Literalism That Kills," *Christian Century Theology*, August 10, 2009]

7. *Ibid.*

8. John Dominic Crossan, *Jesus; A Revolutionary Biography* [San Francisco: Harper Collins, 1994], p. 64.

9. Andrew Sullivan, "When Not Seeing, Is Believing," *TIME*, vol. 168, No. 15, October 9, 2006, p. 60.

10. Walter Wink, *Naming the Powers* [Minneapolis: Fortress Press, 1984], p. 85.

11. Words: Sabine Baring-Gould, in *Church Times* 1865. Music: "St. Gertrude," Arthur S. Sullivan, 1871.

12. Donald Blosser, Goshen College [Goshen, Indiana].

13. Elie Wiesel, Commencement Address, Bucknell University, May 17, 2009.

Chapter Five

In Extraordinary Times

1. ADVENT
LUKE 21:25–36
"THE INTRUSION OF GRACE"

1

This first Sunday of Advent begins the Christian Church's annual reminder that for women and men of faith, the measure of nature is overwhelmed by the bounty of God's long-expected grace. The ordinary progression of the seasons is invaded by an extraordinary birth. Many may have longed for this event, but for what the Bethlehem boy grew up to become no one could ever have been fully prepared.

Much of the world, indeed, many of our neighbors, finds sufficient meaning for their lives in the orderly cycles of time: day and night; birth and death; youth-maturity-ageing; spring-summer-fall-winter. For many people the regular passage of time is also enhanced by the gestures of friendship and the loving gifts of family and human connection. These make alive and warm our days; they comfort our nights, and fill our treasure chests with good memories when those whom we have loved are gone.

Some of our neighbors are surely puzzled and a bit curious about what moves us to come into this holy place week-by-week. For here we do what must seem to them some very strange things: here we pray and plead, we confess and celebrate; here we admit that we have not made ourselves, and we acknowledge that we have been commissioned to serve even these curious and puzzled neighbors.

Christians share with them all these opportunities of nature, and the splendid benefits of the seasons, of family ties, and of human presence.

And we share, as well, the hurt and unfairness, the loss and sadness, the unwonted pain and problems to which we all are heir, and the heartache of benefits forgotten.

But women and men of faith, however meager that faith, count on something more important than even the orderly cycles of time and nature. For into all that we share with our puzzled and curious neighbors, now comes Advent, pointing us to God's beneficent response to our distress. Into all of this now comes Advent, pointing us to what God has done to redress all that is amiss in nature, and to remedy what we have despoiled by our sin.

2

Our Advent pointing, waiting, and preparing is fulfilled with the Christmas celebration of the birth of Christ. This nativity calls us to a new and joyful holiness made possible because God was willing to enter our world by way of the risks and perils of a fragile, unattended human birth.

But Advent does not alert us just to the arrival of the manger child. Advent broadcasts the coming of the *whole* Christ. By his birth, and in his living and dying, and rising again, God has set things aright. By his birth, and in his living and dying, and rising again, God has bestowed upon us a forgiveness beyond all reckoning, and has brought us into a family of care and nurture beyond anything we could have imagined.

In the Gospel appointed for today [Lk 21:25–36], Jesus twice announces the coming of our deliverance: "Your redemption is drawing near!" he said. "The Kingdom of God is near!"

Jesus not only announces God's saving gift, he also lives the life in which this so great a benefit comes to pass. And what a life it was. And by the power of Easter Day, what a life it continues to be! Recall some of the key moments in that most saving life:

- the promises of old, toward which all the signposts were pointed;
- his birth in low estate;
- his growing in wisdom and stature, and in divine and human favor;
- his walking the roads of Palestine in dust and danger;
- his teaching about the importance of inner intent;
- his limitless compassion;
- his challenge to presumption and hypocrisy;
- his parables of appeal and reprimand;
- his sponsoring the peaceful way;
- his calling of women and men to be his friends;

- his shattering of the old norms of social approval;
- his betrayal and criminal execution;
- and the resurrection at the last, in which all that went before finds divine confirmation.

For without his rising to life again, and his continuing presence in the lives and gatherings of the faithful, no one would ever have written the story of the filling-full birth in Bethlehem, toward which we now move in this most blessed season.

3

And so in these Advent Sundays we are invited to remember and to embrace the whole Christ, in whom God has joined heaven and earth. In the face of our trespass and habit of self, God has shown in him just how holy and precious our humanity has become.

The whole Christ toward whose coming Advent points us is God's new picture of what the supremely lived human life looks like. This is God's assurance that, despite all appearances to the contrary, the universe really is on the side of love and justice.

For Jesus was not just a wise teacher *sent* by God to remedy and mend the mess of our distrust. In the whole life of Jesus, God *went* to our world of fractured hopes to make all things new.

Because of this astounding event, we move in Advent toward Christmas Day with amazement and great wonder. Advent is not named to give us time to get ready for a holiday party. Advent will bring us to Christmas on our knees, in reverent acknowledgement of the mystery of God's loving condescension.

This divine gesture assures us of a most surprising state of affairs—that God should so care for us that God accepts us just as we are—with all our weakness and neurosis and sin, so that we might be raised to share in that divine life begun with the birth of Mary's Son.

This is not our reward or our due from God. "It is nothing we have earned. It is not a payment for services well done. . . . It is not the grand total at the bottom of a payslip. . . . [We have heard and learned from Christ that] God is no paymaster or employer or cashier ready to settle accounts. God is [the one] whose privilege and enjoyment it is to give freely and to be merciful." [Karl Barth][1]

Advent does not leave us puzzled or curious, like our wistful neighbors, but overwhelmed, astonished, and amazed at the ingenuity and the measureless generosity of God.

2. ADVENT
MATTHEW 24:36–44
"THE DISTANT SCENE"

1

Getting from one day to the next is not always an easy thing to do. People have come up with various ways to deal with that unease. It helps sometimes to take a deep breath, and then recall one of the words whose wisdom we have come to trust.

Sometimes it is enough to remember that "this too shall pass." Or to say to ourselves, "Be grateful for what you already have." And there is always the cautionary note, "Take one day at a time."

That advice is very much like a line from "Lead, Kindly Light." This is the hymn John Henry Cardinal Newman wrote in 1833. It is seldom sung these days, and it is not in most current hymnals:

> "Lead, kindly light, amidst the encircling gloom. Lead thou me on.
> . . . I do not ask to see the distant scene. One step enough for me."
> "I do not ask to see the distant scene. One step enough for me."

Some of the people who have the hardest time getting from one day to the next are those who are struggling with some form of addiction that can threaten our wellbeing or our ability simply to function. All who struggle with addiction, or whose friends or family members face this problem, know how the journey into health requires us "to take one day at a time," requires us not to "ask to see the distant scene," for "one step" is "enough."

There is a deep wisdom in this cautious way to transcend the ills that trouble us sometimes: "one day at a time," "one step enough for me." That may be the very best that our unbelieving friends and neighbors can manage to do.

But Advent sounds a Gospel note that reduces the worry of such a cautionary life. On this First Sunday of Advent we are given permission to see how faith offers something more than simply one day, one step at a time. Advent recalls us to the promise that pure, empty waiting can give way to a different kind of waiting—not waiting fearfully, but waiting with confidence that God will redeem all that we have entrusted to him.

Those who believe are waiting for the healing visitation of divine grace that is sure to come. For God's grace has brought us this far already, and fills all of our next steps with hope, and with the unfailing company of that great cloud of witnesses who cheer us on, every day and night.

2

The odd and somewhat fearful parable in today's Gospel reading [Mth 24:36–44] ends with the time-rescuing promise: "The Son of Man is coming . . . !"

But in the meantime there is always work to do. This waiting and watching time that Advent symbolizes is not given to us so that we might sit on our hands.

St. Matthew has crafted his version of the Jesus story to make this clear. Three stories follow today's warning about being alert and ready. These familiar stories are the very last three times that Jesus teaches in his public ministry. They are three parables, three tales of lost opportunities, three examples of unfaithful watching and waiting:

In the Parable of Missing Out on the Wedding Reception, or the Parable of the Wise and Foolish Women, five attendants were so foolish as to have brought no oil for their lamps. They discover that they were not guaranteed a place at the party, and the reception begins without them.

In the Parable of the Talent Reckoning, or the Parable of the Talents, one servant/slave buries his master's assets that he should have invested or somehow used to his master's advantage, and is severely reprimanded when his master returns.

In the Parable of the Incognito Christ, the king denounces those who have aided only the people whom they thought deserved their care, but who had ignored those whom Jesus called "the least of these, my brothers and sisters."

And they were all surprised. And their surprise reminds us of one of the persistent dilemmas of Christian faith:

- how to wait, to look ahead, to expect, to be open to the surprising, how to live toward the future, the distant scene,
- and at the same time, to be responsible for what is at hand, to be faithful now to those with whom our lives are bonded, to live with care in the present. For human indifference to need and promise is the great moral failure.

We are called to do these two things at the same time: to be aware of what we have, and to be alert to what God can make possible for us; to live in the *now* and in the *not yet*.

It is as if faith gives us each a pair of bifocals, so that we can see more clearly both the near and the far away, to take the one step that we can take, because Advent brings the distant scene closer than we have thought.

The writer Nikki Giovanni put it this way in a letter to one of her friends:

"There is always something to do. There are hungry people to feed, naked people to clothe, sick people to comfort and make well. And while I don't expect you to save the world, I do think it's not asking too much for you to love those with whom you sleep, [and] to share the happiness of those you call friends."[2]

The language of the Prayer Book puts that sentiment in a more traditional way. In one of the Collects, we acknowledge "that we know not what a day may bring forth, but that the hour for loving God and serving our neighbor is always at hand."

3

And so it is that for people of faith, our time of waiting, our "one day at a time" is not filled with fear or unease.

Uncertainty there may be. The distant scene may not be very clear. But there should by no disabling worry, since our future, however long or short it may be, is the time God has for us.

For God has loved us into life, and is there at our birth and at our death.

By God's grace, we can say "One step enough for me." By God's grace we can live "one day at a time."

In his hymn, Cardinal Newman announces that he does "not ask to see the distant scene." In this Advent season, let us share that view. For like him, we know that something of this "distant scene" has already been revealed to us. That claim is clear in his last verse:

> "So long thy power hath blest me, sure it still will lead me on,
> O'er moor and fen, o'er crag and torrent, till the night is gone;
> And with the morn those angel faces smile,
> Which I have loved long since, and lost awhile."

Among our good friends who have died recently is Bill Coffin. He was a fellow student along with Wanda and me at Yale Divinity School. Bill later became the Yale University Chaplain, and gained national prominence for his involvement in the struggle for civil rights in the View Nam era. During his last and fatal illness earlier this year, he was interviewed by Bill Moyers, who asked him whether he was afraid to die. This was his reply: "I don't know *what* is waiting for me after death. But I do know *who*."[3]

The one thing all persons of faith know for sure about the tomorrow for which we wait, is that God's providence will rise, long before even the sun.

3. ADVENT
PHILIPPIANS 4:4–7
"NEVERTHELESS, REJOICE!"

1

In the Epistle for this third Sunday in Advent [Phil 4:4–7] St. Paul directs us to do something that most people wish we could do, but find it very hard to do. He tells us not "to worry," not to be "anxious," and always "to rejoice." Three short sentences from his happy letter to the little band of Jesus believers gathered in the Greek city of Philippi give us this invitation:

"Rejoice in the Lord always; again I will say, Rejoice. . . . The Lord is near. Do not worry about anything."

We wonder sometimes: does St. Paul live on the same planet where we live? Is he really serious about this advice? Does St. Paul not know how uncertain, how threatened, how near the edge so many people really are? What are we supposed to do when worrisome things happen?

We are glad, of course, when good things turn up, but "rejoice always?" The realities of life as most of us know them to be most of the time, make that invitation almost wishful thinking.

The world just does not appear to us as St. Paul sees it. The world just cannot give birth to or support the rejoicing style of life that St. Paul recommends.

The world we know about just cannot be the source or the guarantor of the rejoicing and the worry-free life of which St. Paul speaks.

And we are absolutely right! The glory and the freight of the world cannot secure our happiness now, or in the age to come.

2

But the joy that St. Paul describes is not based on what we see when we look around at things, or reflect on our life and life of others we know or know about. The rejoicing that St. Paul prescribes is not given by the world, or supported by the world. The joy that St. Paul describes is a defiant "nevertheless." [Karl Barth]

We live and move from one day to the next by the power of faith's great "nevertheless."

We see children neglected and promises broken. We watch dishonesty rewarded, and feel the hurt of benefits forgotten. But *nevertheless*, "We rejoice in the Lord always."

We see loneliness unattended. We have friends who are tired and tired of. We grieve for deaths out-of-order, and the pain of promises broken. But *nevertheless*, "We rejoice in the Lord always."

We see heavy demands on food banks, weeping families of the war dead and wounded. We feel the despair of the abused and overworked. But *nevertheless*, "We rejoice in the Lord always."

3

Where does this startling bravado of faith come from? Whence this protest of belief?

The defiant "nevertheless" that moves us to rejoice in spite of unfairness on every hand, is not authorized by the world and its power to confer life and death. It is chartered by the constant presence of Christ.

In him God has invaded this world, and destroyed its power to destroy the satisfactions of our loves, and the profit of all our effort to reduce misery and dire wont.

The source of this great defiant "nevertheless" that moves us to rejoice always, "in spite of" the way and the weight of the world, has been named by St. Paul in today's Epistle: "the Lord is near." And this Lord will one day say to his disciples: "In the world you shall have tribulation; but be of good cheer; I have overcome the world." [Jn 16:33]

The Gospel writers framed their story of Jesus with the challenging declaration of God's messengers. The angelic announcement on the hills outside Bethlehem and outside the Tomb of Joseph defines forever the immensity of faith's great "nevertheless."

To the startled shepherds keeping watch over their flock by night, the angel or messenger of the Lord said, "Fear not; for behold I bring you good tidings of great joy . . ." [Lk 2:10]

To the surprised women standing before the sepulcher outside Jerusalem's walls, the angel or messenger of the Lord said, "Fear not; for I know that you seek Jesus, which was crucified. He is not here; for he is risen." [Mth 28:5–6]

4

The birth and rebirth that the angelic heralds announce provide the envelope within which is lived the life of him -

- who overcomes the world of grasping, and blesses receiving instead;
- who breaks the hold of our ultimate worries;

- who confers the great joy of our knowing that "all will be well";
- who endows a peace unlike any worldly armistice.

To the consternation and great puzzlement of our curious and wistful neighbors, the One Who Comes and Who Overcomes the rule of the world makes the defiant "nevertheless" possible

We "rejoice in the Lord always" because we know that our life is no longer determined by possessions, by stuff, by what we have or do not have. We "rejoice in the Lord always" because we know that our life is no longer secured by what we have earned, but by what we have been given:

- a forgiveness beyond expectation;
- a family exceeding blood and imagination;
- a peace that surpasses our dreams;
- a grace that has no measure.

This is the Promised Life of Advent that we rescue from the past and make our own every time we gather in this holy room. Sharing the broken bread and outpoured wine at this altar does not just rekindle our memories, it fills our present with his glad-making presence.

The happy letter-writer to the Philippian Christians who asked us to "Rejoice in the Lord always," would, it seems to me, agree with one of our better contemporary playwrights, Paul Rudnick. Fr. Dan, the priest in Rudnick's play *Jeffrey*, captures the obligation of the Epistle and the blessed permission of the Gospel in one of his most dramatic lines: "There is only one real blasphemy," he said, "the refusal of joy."[4]

4. CHRISTMAS
LUKE 2:1–20 KJV
"THE PONDER HEART"

"And Mary kept all these things and pondered them in her heart." [Lk 2:19 KJV]

1

The saving burden that this first Mass of Christmas lays upon us is signaled by the last words of today's Gospel [Lk 2:1–20 KJV]. This is St. Luke's closing comment about the woman on whom this story depends, and thus about the woman on whom our faith depends: "And Mary kept all these things, and pondered them in her heart."

She "pondered" these things in her heart! As well she might. For she had a lot to ponder. She had a lot to think about.

Here she is—a Jewish teenager, betrothed but not yet living with her husband, and dealing with an unplanned pregnancy, what her family, her friends and neighbors would have regarded as an out-of-wedlock pregnancy. A life-threatening plight in those days. A lot to ponder indeed!

Joseph apparently had a handyman trade. But like all the other Palestinian Jewish peasants, he and Mary were dirt poor. They were made so by the oppressive tax policies of the Roman occupation. And the heavy demands of their collaborators in the priesthood attached to the great Jerusalem Temple made matters even worse.

And now they are forced by that regime to travel from Nazareth, not far from the Golan Heights in the North, all the way to Jerusalem. That is about like walking from Hamilton to Binghamton—in the winter.

This difficult journey was to comply with the Roman government's call for a census, or taxation, or official registration of some sort. And now Mary has given birth in a smelly barn, with only Joseph's help, and with animals and cow dung all around.

But she survived. Not just somehow! She survived with courage, and with the confidence that neither God nor her husband had abandoned her.

2

We do not know, of course, what came to her mind when Mary "kept all these things, and pondered them in her heart." She could hardly have guessed how the story begun with the angel's promise would come out.

Whoever, eighty years later, put the finishing touches on St. Luke's Gospel, could only have begun to see the full significance of Mary's little boy.

Who could have known that the baby in the stable would so live and die and live again that the life of the world would be changed forever!

Who could have known that the child in the barn would be the one to show, more clearly than anyone ever before, how we might live out responsibly and lovingly the time and space God has given to us for a while!

Mary "kept all these things and pondered them in her heart," but she could not have known what St. Luke knew—that the cross and the empty tomb would one day fulfill the promise of that nativity "in royal David's city."

The grown-up Jesus—betrayed, executed, buried, and raised to a transformed and transforming life again—the grown-up Jesus rescued those who were hurt by the lack of charity. He healed those who were abused by the cruel indifference of those around them. And what he did must be the mandate for the gatherings of women and men who take his name as their own.

The grown-up Jesus welcomed those who are shut out of family and friends because they cannot make themselves acceptable to other persons. He did not care where they had been or where they were coming from. There is room for all. "In my Father's house," he will say, "there are many mansions." And what he promised must be the program for the gathering of women and men who take his name as their own.

As she pondered the glorious mysteries of this night, Mary may have worried that the barn in Bethlehem might lead to a cross on Golgotha, outside the walls of Jerusalem. But St. Luke did not wonder. He knew that this indeed would come to pass.

Because of what the infant Jesus grew up to say and to do, and to be, we know, that despite all appearances to the contrary, the universe really is on the side of the women and men who aim to heal the unease of those who are hurt.

Because of what the infant Jesus grew up to say and to do, and to be, we know, that despite all appearances to the contrary, our making a turn to the other who needs us is the highest calling of all who take the name of Christ as their own.

Because of what the infant Jesus grew up to say and to do, and to be, we know that despite all appearances to the contrary, a life-policy of caring—even at great cost—is the true mark of a faithful life. Standing and embracing, weeping and laughing with one another may be purpose enough.

3

To gather in this holy place this night, and to hear once again the Christmas Gospel, is to be invited to do what Mary did: to ponder the sacred mysteries of God's taking on the human face of Mary's Son for the eternal benefit of the whole human family.

St. Luke reports that the angels finished their song and departed. The shepherds left the stable and returned to their flocks and fields.

We too will soon leave behind the poetry, the pictures, the music, and go back to the prose and the hassles of our homes. But if we do Mary's thing, and "ponder" these sacred events, we will receive a boon beyond our imagining.

We may sing "Glory to God in the highest." But something else happens when we ponder the difference that the incarnation of God makes for a world of pained and struggling people. This is the Very Body of Christ, born in the stable, suffered on the cross, and shared on this altar.

If the Bethlehem birth of the Christ does not overcome our obsession with self, then let the self-offering of Christ in this and every Eucharist move us to minister to a wounded world, and to comfort a betrayed heart.

If the Bethlehem birth of the Christ does not shame our reluctance to serve, then let the self-offering of Christ in this and every Eucharist move us to assuage a guilty conscience, and to forgive a broken promise.

Then, perhaps, we will not gasp and have to pause or to hurry on when we pray for God to "forgive us our trespasses, *as we forgive those who trespass against us."*

May it be our deepest wish that amidst all the giving and receiving of Christmas Day, each of us might cherish most the gift of a "ponder heart."

With a "ponder heart" we will know there is no abyss in our life so deep but has a bottom.

With a "ponder heart" we will praise the God who in Christ opens windows and doors for us, just when we thought our past mistakes had shut us up forever.

With a "ponder heart" we will rest eternally secure in the arms of the One who assures us in Mary's Child that long before the day begins, the sun of God's generous good pleasure will already have arisen.

5. EPIPHANY
MATTHEW 2:1–12
"WITH THE LENS OF THE INCARNATION"

1

Like many of you, my wife and I have put Christmas away. We have packed up the decorations, boxed up the candles. We have set aside the basket of Christmas cards and letters for one more reading when the snow comes. We have disconnected the flood light that shone on the tall blue spruce that our daughter Martha helped me plant in the front of the house when she was three. Then we put the now denuded Christmas tree out by the curb for the Hamilton village pick up.

But there is a piece of Christmas that we have not boxed up and put away until next December. And that is the new set of glasses that we have been given by the Incarnation of God in the life of Jesus of Nazareth.

I hope very much that each of you received a pair of these special clarifying Christmas glasses as well.

Jesus' life and death and rising to life again has given us this new lens, this new way of seeing everything and everybody. This new pair of glasses makes it possible for us to look in a new way at ourselves and at one another; a new way of regarding those whom we love and those whom we do not like. A new way of seeing what we have been given, of regarding the stranger who knocks on our door, the newcomer whom we meet.

These new glasses are fitted with the lens of the Incarnation. This is the way of looking that takes seriously what has happened to our life because God's embracing Word became flesh and dwelt among us.

2

That this time-dividing event is a boon for the whole human family, and not just for Jesus' biological kinfolk, is confirmed by the two Gospel stories of Jesus' birth. They share many important features, but they point to the outreaching nature of faith in different ways.

St. Luke's story was the Gospel for Christmas Eve. Here Joseph and Mary live in Nazareth in the northern part of Palestine, and travel to Bethlehem, down near Jerusalem, so that Joseph can take part in a census ordered by the occupying Roman authorities. They find temporary lodgings in a stable where Jesus is born.

That birth is soon attended to by some shepherds. These are the outsiders, the workers, the marginal folk of that day. They are the ones identified in Mary's song, as "those of low degree," whom God will raise up.

St. Matthew's story was the Gospel for Epiphany. Here Joseph and Mary are living in Bethlehem. And Jesus is born in their house. That birth is soon attended to by the Magi, the so-called "wise men," very likely Persian astrologer-priests who had followed a star to the house. These are the outsiders of a different sort; they stand for the whole non-Jewish world, as well as all those of high degree in Mary's song, whom God will put down.

Yet thirty years later no one seemed to know just who it was that would heal the human heart, and make a new way of being God's people possible, except perhaps for Mary. The shepherds had gone back to watching their flocks. The wise-men had returned to their homes in the East. Both disappear completely from the Jesus story, and are never heard of again. Except perhaps for Mary, no one seems to know what is so special about this Man from Nazareth, or what difference he is going to make. No one, that is, until the announcement at Jesus' baptism by John:

". . . when Jesus . . . had been baptized . . . a voice came from heaven, 'You are my Son, the Beloved; with you I am well pleased.'"

The heavenly voice does not announce a moral disciplinarian to increase our guilt, or a critic to lower our self-esteem and encourage self-pity.

The heavenly voice does not announce a visitor from some other realm to amaze us with his tricks.

To use the rather extravagant language of a fourth century Christian mystic, the heavenly voice announces one who became like us, so that we might become like him.

3

The Epiphany season on which we have now entered gives a special slant on what we are to make of the Incarnation—the arrival of God's Son, the Beloved, with whom God is well-pleased.

We have a clue in our ordinary way of talking. We sometimes speak of experiencing epiphanies in our own life, even if we never use the term "epiphany." After puzzling something out, we might say "Oh, now I get the point." Or "Now I see it," or "Now it finally makes sense." Those are all epiphany moments.

This is what the birth and life, the death and the rising to life again of the Beloved Son makes possible for us. It gives us the clue that unlocks the puzzle, or that sheds light on the story of our life, or gives us the new lenses of our Incarnation glasses.

Every Eucharistic Prayer witnesses to this dramatic donation of new vision. But this is suggested most clearly in Eucharistic Prayer B in Rite 2. In the beginning of that prayer, the narrative refers to several strategies that God had used for conveying to humankind the picture of what our life really could be:

The goodness and love disclosed in creation. But that became marred and spoiled.

The calling of a family to be God's people [not the modern nation State of Israel, but the ancient people of Israel]. But they turned their gift and task into a privilege.

The Word spoken through the prophets. But no one listened.

Finally, in the Word made flesh: bringing us "out of sin into righteousness, out of death into life," and in the language of Epiphany, "out of darkness into light."

4

God's taking on a human face in the Beloved Son gives us this new lens through which we can look on all the things and beings that meet us, and on all the events we share.

Through the lens of the Incarnation, we can see the hand of God in every increment of justice, and in every grant of forgiveness.

Through the lens of the Incarnation, we can see that no one is irredeemable.

Through the lens of the Incarnation, we can see that we all have been given another chance.

Through the lens of the Incarnation, we can see what a holy thing our humanity has become. And then we will pray that this vision of holiness will move us to rescue the lost, and to care unconditionally for all those whom we love. This part of Christmas we must not put away.

Then may it be that a voice from heaven will say of God's other sons and daughters, "With you I am well pleased."

6. EPIPHANY
JOHN 1:29–42
"WHERE ARE YOU STAYING, JESUS?"

1

The Church is one of the few remaining avenues left by which we can recover some of the life-saving gifts of our past. Our readings each week from the Old and New Testaments, open up one of the best of these roads to the resources of our past. These readings help us to keep in touch with the blessings, the promises, the reprimands, the comforts, the reassurances of that great cloud of witnesses who continue to cheer us on as we strive for the high-calling God offers us in the career of Christ.

We read from the Gospels, and are reminded of the beginnings of our faith; but we have come here to have our spirits renewed, not to satisfy our historical curiosity.

We read the story of the ancient Israelites, and recall the vision of the prophets and celebrate the assurance of the Psalms; but we have come here to find more peace for our lives, not to acquire more information.

We read the letters of St. Paul, and are reminded of the surprising courage of the earliest companies of believers; but we have come here to have our sympathies deepened, not to have our memories awakened.

But now and then something turns up in one of the appointed lessons that informs us about our past, about the beginnings of our faith tradition, and, at the same time, has special importance for our lives in this very present.

2

In today's Gospel [Jn 1:29–42] we hear two questions. The Gospel story turns on these questions, but the story of our own lives may also turn on these questions.

These questions occur in the conversation reported by St. John between Jesus and two of the disciples or followers of John the Baptist. John the Baptist had launched a preaching campaign against the religious establishment, vigorously denouncing what he regarded as corruption in its very heart, and especially the way the chief priests colluded with the Roman occupation authorities.

John called for individual and national repentance. He looked for some new, definitive act of God on behalf of the people. And now he senses that this hoped-for divine intervention has begun with Jesus, whom he names the "Lamb of God," and finally the "Son of God."

Two of John's disciples overhear him speak this way about Jesus, and so they turn to him. Perhaps he might be what was missing in John's program. Jesus notices their interest, and asks them a question that probes their anxiety and our own: "What are you looking for?"

They do not know what to say. Perhaps they do not even know how to name what is missing in their life.

Their leader, John the Baptist, had spoken of Jesus in a strange way: "Here is the Lamb of God who takes away the sin of the world." Nobody had ever said that before. Perhaps Simon and Andrew thought they had better check this out.

Their leader, John the Baptist, had used extraordinary language when he identified Jesus. Not enough to say Jesus is the "Lamb of God." John raises the bar as high as it can go, when he added, "I have testified that this is the Son of God." Perhaps Simon and Andrew thought they had better see for themselves.

And so they reply to Jesus with a question of their own. Jesus had asked them, "What are you looking for?" "You seem to be following me. Has John's words about my being "Lamb of God" and "Son of God" piqued your interest? Are you looking for how God's new call to holiness might change your life?"

Simon and Andrew respond by asking, "Where are you staying?"

3

That was their question to Jesus: "Where are you staying?" Our words may be different, but we ask the same question: "Where can we find this One who forgives our sins and misadventures, who comforts our unease, who empowers us always to regard the other as our kin"?

Jesus responded to John's curious disciples with one of the most promising invitations in all the New Testament: "Come and see!" He responds to our question by making the same offer.

John's disciples "came and saw where he was staying, and they stayed with him that day." The door is open for us to do the same.

[a] We do not know where Jesus was staying that day with his two new disciples. But we do know some of the places where he has promised us to be:

We can meet him right here in this holy place, as the bread is broken and the wine poured out. For at this table we experience the most radical sharing we are likely ever to have.

Here we receive a family of sisters and brothers beyond our imagining. Here we share in a company of equals who have given up any need to feel superior.

Here we belong to a company of forgiven and forgiving sinners. Here we join in a community of folks who have been given to one another by him who gives himself to us, and who wants only to call us friends.

[b] We do not know where Jesus was staying that day with his two new disciples. But we do know some of the places where he has promised us to be:

We will meet him wherever compassion replaces the urge to condemn. We will meet him wherever justice-making replaces satisfaction with the way things are.

We will meet him wherever hospitality replaces hostility, and patience outlasts the loss of hope.

And we will meet him wherever our desire to get from God what we truly deserve gives way to gratitude for God's blessings that surpass anything that we could ever have earned.

"Where are you staying, Jesus?"

"Come and see."

7. TRANSFIGURATION
MATTHEW 17:1–9
"TRANSFIGURATIONS"

1

Epiphany ends as it began: a voice from the clouds announces that Jesus is God's Beloved Son. On the First Sunday of Epiphany we read of Jesus' baptism when the words are addressed to Jesus: "*You* are my Beloved Son; with you I am well pleased." [Mk 1:11] Today, on this last Sunday of Epiphany, the words are addressed to the terrified inner circle of his disciples: *"This* is my Son, the Beloved." [Mth 17:1–9; // Mk 9:2–8, Lk 9:28–36]

The *first* reassures Jesus as he begins his public career of rebuking the greedy, welcoming the abandoned, attending to the wounded whom others ignore, and giving voice to those who have no one to speak for them. The *last* authorizes and instructs the disciples to pay attention to God's Beloved Son, to trust his directives, and to conform their lives to his. "Now that you know who this man is," the heavenly voice says, "Listen to him!"

To listen to him and to say of him that he is "God's Son, the Beloved," is to say nothing about his biological origin, but to say everything about the saving grace he brings to humankind.

To hear the announcement that Jesus is "God's Son, the Beloved," is to acknowledge and to endeavor to live by the way of God that was embodied in Jesus, as in no other.

To say of Jesus that he is "God's Son, the Beloved," is to acknowledge what a holy thing our humanity has become because of him.

To say of Jesus that he is "the Beloved Son of God," is not just a way to get our theology right, although we surely will want to do that. We call Jesus "the Beloved Son of God," not because we want to speak well of him, but because we want to listen to him, and to follow his way as best we can—the way of including and touch; the way of justice-seeking and compassion-sharing; the way of peace-making and mercy-giving. Perhaps then, as we listen and follow, he might, at the end, think well of us.

2

One of the Gospel accounts of Jesus' Transfiguration is always appointed for the last Sunday after the Epiphany. The Transfiguration is a very peculiar story, although the basic features of the tale are quite simple: as Jesus is praying in the hills, his whole appearance is changed. It becomes shining, bright, radiant. His three close friends, who had gone with him up into the hills, are awe-struck, frightened.

As well they might be. For they had just shared the rarest of human experiences. They had witnessed the transforming, radiant glory of God. Their lives would never be the same.

Our lives, too, are changed by our encounters with the holy transcendence of God. But most of us meet that shining holiness in much less dramatic ways than did Peter, James and John.

The voice from the clouds says of Jesus that he is "God's Son, the Beloved." To have our ordinary human life invested with such holiness means that God's grace now meets us in the most ordinary occasions of our life. We need not wait or look for the shattering, resplendent mountain-top experiences.

For the shining radiance of God meets us sometimes in the most unspectacular ways: in our friendships and loves; in our blessed memories; in moments of caring and being cared for; in doing all the necessary work of the world so that we can keep on keeping on.

3

Thinking this way about transfigurations is confirmed by the Greek text of the New Testament. Except for a few Aramaic terms, all of the Gospels and letters in the New Testament, indeed, all the surviving Christian literature from the first century were written in Greek. I seldom make reference to features of the Greek text from the pulpit, but a quick glance today might suggest how the Transfiguration story of Jesus might affect the transfiguration stories of our life.

When Matthew writes of Jesus' Transfiguration, he uses the same word that other New Testament authors use when they refer to the influence of Jesus Christ in the life of the believer. It is the root of the word "metamorphosis," the most radical transformation in the natural world.

In his letter to the Christians in Rome, St. Paul identified what kind of change can happen to those who listen to God's Son, the Beloved One. It is a transfiguration as momentous as what Jesus' experienced, and as awesome as what his little group of friends shared.

"Be not conformed any longer to the pattern of this world," Paul wrote, "but be transformed [changed, transfigured] by the renewing of your mind, so that you may discern what is the will of God." [Rom 12:2]

Be not conformed to the pattern of this world, but be changed, transfigured in the presence of God's Son, the Beloved One, no longer supposing that what we have or do not have finally matters.

Be not conformed to the pattern of this world, but be changed, transfigured in the presence of God's Son, the Beloved One, no longer trying to decide which of the needy deserves our care.

Be not conformed to the pattern of this world, but be changed, transfigured in the presence of God's Son, the Beloved One, no longer thinking that the social graces are more important than social justice.

Be not conformed to the pattern of this world, but be changed, transfigured in the presence of God's Son, the Beloved One, no longer letting a concern for the new and the interesting trump our devotion to duty.

4

At Jesus' Baptism and at his Transfiguration, the heavenly voice says to him and of him that this self-offering, other-disposed man is God's Beloved Son. With that blessing and with that authority he will soon say of himself, "I am the Way, the Truth, and the Life."

The heavenly voice begs his friends, and begs us as well, to "Listen to him." We will do that as best we can. Then it may be that someday we will hear a voice from heaven say to us, "You are my daughters and sons, my beloved ones. With you I am well pleased."

8. LENT
JOHN 3:1–17
"THE WRITING ON THE WALL"

1

First—two stories, a back way into today's Gospel. [Jn 3:1–17]

Many years ago I spent some summer weeks in Le Chambon, a largely Huguenot or Protestant village in the South of France. This is the village whose people successfully hid several hundred Jewish children during the Nazi occupation of France. This gospel-sponsored effort was led by the Protestant pastors, whose large, rectangular church stood in the center of town.

Its interior walls were quite plain, except for the front wall facing the congregation. In true Huguenot fashion, there was no altar, since the sermon was the main event in the service. And so the main focus was on the very large pulpit, behind and above which there was painted in large black letters an important biblical verse. Those sacred words confronted, inspired, and challenged every person who came there to worship.

That verse, inescapably visible to everyone, helps to explain the villagers' faith-driven actions in sheltering endangered children during the war, and managing to get many of them to safety in Switzerland.

The biblical words that faced every worshipper at every service were these [in French of course]: "The Master is here, and calleth for thee."

That text is from St. John's Gospel account of the raising of Lazarus. [Jn 11:28] We will hear the full story on the Sunday next before Palm Sunday. Jesus has arrived in Bethany to be with his friends Martha and Mary on the death of their brother Lazarus. He speaks to Martha first, and then Martha seeks out her sister, and says to her," The Master is here, and calleth for thee." [KJV]

Those words became the Gospel announcement to every worshipper at the Le Chambon Huguenot Church. No matter what else was said or done, Martha's words to Mary became the Church's regular words to all who came to pray:

"The Master is here and calleth for thee"—not for solace alone, but for energy to do the work of the kingdom.

"The Master is here and calleth for thee"—not for comfort alone, but for the high commission to do the works of justice, always and at whatever cost.

"The Master is here and calleth for thee"—not just for personal profit, but for public gain.

"The Master is here and calleth for thee." Imagine how our life might be improved by a weekly reminder of that holy invitation.

2

A second story. I grew up in the northern Indiana city of Goshen. A highpoint of my senior high school year was our debate team's trip to Indianapolis, to compete in a state-wide tournament.—my very first trip to the state capital.

On Sunday morning of that weekend, I attended the early service at Christ Church, the cathedral for the Indianapolis Episcopal Diocese. I remember very little of that service, but I recall quite clearly what every worshipper saw at every service in that holy space. Inscribed in large, Gothic script, on the vast archway over the choir and aisle leading up to the high altar, was this verse from St. John's Gospel [in the King James version, of course]: "Neither do I condemn thee; go and sin no more."

Those who made this selection long ago in Indianapolis certainly chose one of the great biblical texts: "Neither do I condemn thee; go and sin no more." [Jn 8:11]

To be greeted at every service with those life-giving words would nourish a worshipper with serious Gospel truth.

For these words of Jesus to the woman accused and judged by self-righteous men underscore what the Church always announces whenever it is true to itself. The Gospel proclamation is not to increase our guilt, but to free us from all self-condemnation.

This liberation does not endow our comfort; it seeks to amend our life. This kind of forgiveness sends us on our way—determined no longer by our mistakes, bound no more by our bad choices, but washed clean in a great cascade of compassion.

"Neither do I condemn thee; go and sin no more." Imagine how our life might be improved by a weekly reminder of that holy generosity.

3

End of stories! The kind of church architecture and design that involved painting scriptural texts on a wall has largely gone out of style. And I am not campaigning for its revival.

But one aspect of such a project has always intrigued me—how do people go about choosing the biblical words to use? That would be a challenging assignment indeed.

We would surely want such a text to state somehow the main message of the Gospel. Any text that we would inscribe on the church walls, would surely need to be a text that would be so central to faith that we would want it to be inscribed as well on our hearts and etched in our memories. Seeing it at every service would guide our life by its wisdom, and so we would need to choose carefully.

The Gospel appointed for today offers us such a likely choice. Here we find the most frequently cited capsule of the good news: "For God so loved the world that he gave his only Son, so that everyone who believes in him may not perish but may have eternal life." [Jn 3:16]

Many of you will recognize this as one of the "Comfortable Words" in the old liturgy, and retained in Rite 1. Martin Luther called this passage "the Gospel *in nuce*," "The Gospel in a nutshell."

To see those words at every service would nourish a worshipper with serious Gospel truth, no matter what else was said or done. For all we need to know is here: the reminder that this very world of sinful straying has been loved with a measureless love; that this very world of unthinking cruelty and unfairness has been visited by the One who heals and restores.

All we need to know is here: the assurance that we have been forgiven, even in advance, and without anybody counting.

And all this by the One who in Jesus Christ has thrown away the account books, and the ledgers of good deeds and bad.

All we need to know is here; that we are being renewed, and that not for our private satisfaction, but to give us warrant for compassion so that we might turn toward the other.

4

We do not need to write any of the great texts of the Bible on the church walls. But it behooves us to write them on our hearts:

"The Master is here and calleth for thee."

"Neither do I condemn thee; go and sin no more."

"For God so loved the world that he gave his only Son, so that everyone who believes in him may not perish, but may have eternal life."

9. LENT
JOHN 9:1–27
"FAITH AS A WAY OF SEEING"

1

Being a Christian believer is never easy. Our cynical friends and indifferent neighbors have already given up. They are probably shaking their heads with some amusement when they see what we do on Sunday morning.

They do have a point. Believing in the goodness and the generous love of God does not come without some effort in our world. There is so much around us that is mean and unfair, so much that is cruel and unfeeling.

But each of the readings appointed for this Fourth Sunday in Lent points us to a way of thinking about faith, and living a life of faith, that might make it more plausible to be a Christian believer.

Faith, after all, is a way of seeing things and people, long before it is a way of thinking and talking. A new way of looking at life, long before we turn to creeds and doctrines and theology, important as these special words really are.

The great gift of faith is not certainty, but insight. The great gift of faith is not freedom from doubt, but freedom to love. The great gift of faith is not a new set of doctrines to embrace, but a new vision by which to live.

If our unknowing friends and unsympathetic neighbors knew that having our faith nourished is what we seek when we come into this holy house, they might be more understanding. They might then be less puzzled and more sympathetic, perhaps even a bit envious.

2

Consider the different ways in which today's biblical writers picture faith as a special way of seeing, long before it issues in creeds and doctrines.

The author of the Books of Samuel does this in the form of a story. [I Sam 16:1–13] Samuel is charged with the task of choosing one of the sons of Jesse to replace the discredited Saul as king. He checks out all of Jesse's older sons, each one of whom Samuel finds impressive, but not quite right.

He finally settles on David. David was not only Jesse's youngest son, but his father thought him so inappropriate and unsuitable that he had not even brought him to Samuel for an interview.

Yet Samuel had the sense that there was something about David that Jesse had not noticed. Not anything about his appearance, but an intuition about his character.

The author speaks about Samuel's recognizing David to be the best choice by using some words that we would all do well to remember: "The Lord does not see as mortals see; they look on the outward appearance, but the Lord looks on the heart."

3

There are hints of this approach in today's Psalm and Epistle as well.

The Twenty-third Psalm is regularly read in the Burial Office. We need to hear its words on occasions like that especially. For the Psalmist gives voice to a way of seeing the death that awaits us all. No longer a terror to be feared, but always an event filled with God's presence. "Though I walk through the valley of the shadow of death, I will fear no evil, for Thou art with me." I am not afraid to die, for "I shall dwell in the house of the Lord forever."

And in the Epistle, St. Paul suggests that believing gives us a new push for pursuing the good, the right, and the true. We have not been called to be children of the light for our benefit alone, he said, but to shed some light on the way for others.

4

St. John makes his point in the form of another story. [Jn 9:1–13 {14–27} 28–38] It is a story of Jesus giving sight to a blind man. The man who was healed is asked to explain just how it all happened. He replies that he does not know. "One thing I do know, that though I was blind, now I see." The climax of this story is surely one of the most dramatic lines in the entire New Testament: "Once I was blind, but now I see." [RSV]

The Pharisees investigating the case and the man whose blindness was healed all saw the same Jesus. But they saw him in different ways. The

Pharisees saw Jesus as a trickster. The once-blind man saw Jesus as the one in whom God had become savingly present to his life. Notice what his last response to Jesus is: "And he worshiped him." Not "Thanks a lot!" St. John says "and he worshiped him."

And his worshipful response tells us that it is not just ordinary seeing that is involved here. In this story, it is a spiritual blindness [or unbelief] that is contrasted with spiritual seeing [or insight]. And the point of the story seems to be something like this:

It takes not only sight, but also insight to recognize Jesus as the bearer of divine compassion.

It takes not only sight, but also insight to accept a heart broken open by love as the deepest truth about human life.

It takes not only sight, but also insight to be open to the God who accepts us in spite of ourselves, who welcomes without charge all of us who could never afford any price of admission.

5

We who believe, however haltingly, live in the same world as our cynical neighbors and indifferent friends. We see the same adversities. We experience the same suffering and cruelty, the same illnesses and misfortunes. But we see this world of misfortune in different ways.

To our cynical neighbors and indifferent friends, bad things happening to good people is just more evidence of divine indifference, or vengeance of the sort that the Pharisees thought caused the blindness of the man in the Gospel story.

But with the eyes of faith, the believer sees such events, bad as they are, but still occasions for God to bring some good to pass. With the eyes of faith, the believer sees whatever happens as an occasion in which God will show us that we are not alone; that in life, in death, and in life beyond death God is with us—reconciling, renewing, sustaining. With the eyes of faith we see that when we are alone, we are *never* alone.

When the hurt and pain, when accidents and injury come our way, let us not ask, "Why did God let this happen to them, to us, or to me?"

Let us ask rather, "How are we to respond in faith to this hurt or this pain, to this reminder of the fragility and the unfairness of human life?"

Let us ask rather, "How is God showing God's grace even in this event?"

For God causes no suffering. But there is no suffering from which God is absent, or that God asks us to endure on our own.

God causes no death, but there is no death that can ever defeat God's compassion. God causes no death, but there is no death that can take away forever the meaning and joy of the life God has given us—for however short or long a time.

Of all the many countless gifts of grace, perhaps the most precious is the permission finally to say, "Once I was blind, blind to God's presence in my life and in our world. Once I was blind, but now I see."

Then may it be said of us, as it was said of the man whose blindness Jesus healed: "And he worshiped him."

10. EASTER DAY
JOHN 20:10–18
"THE RESURRECTION AS GOD'S ENDORSEMENT"

1

If Christ has not been raised, nothing else matters.

On this Easter Day we announce to an unbelieving, anxious, and worried world, "Christ is Risen! He is risen indeed!" But our proclamation is not simply about a Jesus event 20 centuries ago, outside Jerusalem in Roman occupied Palestine. The Easter Day proclamation announces what *our* life can be *now* because of that event. It tells us what *our* life can be *now* if we take this story to heart.

In the Collect, we have prayed "that we may live with him in the joy of his resurrection." In today's Epistle, St. Paul reminds us that "*we* have been raised with Christ." Since Christ is no longer in his grave, we can begin *now* to live the eternal life he brings. Since the Spirit of Christ's so-generous acceptance has been set loose in the world, we can begin now to let go the bad habit of supposing that we have made it on our own, or that we have to make it on our own. "Christ is risen. He is risen indeed!"

The Transfiguration story that we heard on the last Sunday in Epiphany has already given us a clue to the real meaning of this day. In that story, three of Jesus' close disciples hear the divine voice saying of Jesus: "This is my Son, my Chosen. Listen to him." [Lk 9:35]

To listen to the resurrection story is to hear this divine voice testifying to us of Jesus, saying "Raising Jesus and exalting him above all others is my way of telling you that what this Jesus *said* I endorse; that what this Jesus *did* I approve; and that his life policy of love-without-conditions I recommend."

What Jesus said, what he did, and the kind of love he embodies is now vindicated beyond all question by the resurrection. If Christ has been raised, nothing else matters. He is the human face of God. Listen to him.

2

Just what did Jesus say?

"Blessed are the peacemakers, for they will be called children of God." [Mth 5:7]

"Whoever does the will of God is my brother and sister and mother." [Mk 3:35]

"Where your treasure is, there will your heart be also." [Mth 6:21]

"Come unto me, all you that are weary and heavy-laden, and I will give you rest." [Mth 11:28]

"I am the Way, the Truth, and the Life." [Jn 14:6]

By the resurrection, God has confirmed the truth of these words. By the resurrection, God has ratified the life-giving importance of what Jesus said.

Just what did Jesus do?

"And he took the little children up in his arms, laid his hands on them, and blessed them." [Mk 10:16]

"While they were eating, he took a loaf of bread, and after blessing it he broke it, gave it to them, and said, 'Take; eat; this is my Body." [Mth 26:26]

"And the Pharisees and the scribes were grumbling and saying, 'This fellow welcomes sinners and eats with them.'" [Lk 15:2]

And in the words of today's First Lesson: "He went about doing good and healing all who were oppressed." [Acts 10:38]

By the resurrection, God has approved these deeds. By the resurrection, God has recommended this pattern of life.

And just who is this Jesus?

In St. Paul's words: "In him all the fullness of God was pleased to dwell." [Col 12:9]

Jesus' self-affirmation in St. John's Gospel: "The Father and I are one." [Jn 10:30]

The divine voice at Jesus' baptism, according to St. Matthew: "This is my Son, the Beloved, with whom I am well pleased." [Mth 3:17]

By the resurrection, God has verified the claim these words announce. By the resurrection, God has confirmed and vouched for the way the humanity of Jesus was divinely lived.

And so now we know: what Jesus *said* and what Jesus *did*, indeed *who* the early believers recognized Jesus to be—all of this is declared to be true by the resurrection.

3

Many sermons begin by retelling the Gospel story, and then move on to suggest what that might mean for our lives today. But I began by letting St. John's Gospel story stand, and began by considering the meaning of the resurrection of Christ. But now I want to look briefly at some special features of the Gospel story.

For it is in the form of a story that we hear of God's endorsement of who Jesus was, of what he said and did. Each of the four New Testament Gospels tells the story in a different way. We have heard today St. John's account. [Jn 20:10–18] His special insight into the meaning of the resurrection faith comes in the poignant interchange he records between Jesus and Mary Magdalene:

"Jesus said to her, 'Mary.' . . . She turned and said to him, 'My Dear Lord.'" And then moved to embrace him as usual.

Mary was apparently from the town of Magdala on the western shore of the Sea of Galilee, not far from Capernaum. This village was Jesus' base of operations after he had left his home-town of Nazareth.

She has been known in the tradition simply as Mary Magdalene. And the Gospel writers tell us something very important about her. Her presence at the tomb of Jesus is the one thing that all four Gospel narratives have in common.

The Easter story writers give different versions of who was there on that Sunday morning; why they had gone; what they saw and what they heard. But the one person unfailingly mentioned by name as being there is Mary of Magdala.

St. John pictures her as going there alone, sometime between three and six in the morning, while it is still dark.

St. John does not say why Mary visited the tomb, and why she went all alone. But everyone here who has deeply loved knows what drew her there—not to finish the burial arrangements; not to check out forgotten details; not to *do* anything at all.

She goes simply to *be* there in the heartache that all the loving ones of the world understand.

Her grief is answered by Jesus' speaking to her by name. He not only comforts and reassures her. He sends her on a mission, giving her a task to do: to tell his other followers that she "had seen the Lord." To tell the others that God has acknowledged Jesus as his Son, and has ratified and endorsed all that he had said and done.

4

Jesus' compassion and presence with Mary, his supporter and disciple, had enabled her to become her true and better self. And now she is the very first witness of the risen Jesus. Jesus' appearance to her in the garden confirms the risen life she had already begun to live by virtue of Jesus' care.

I said earlier that the New Testament gives us four Easter Day stories. But most of us in this sacred space know that there are not just four.

There are as many resurrection stories as there are women and men who find themselves delivered from the prison of bad habits. There are as many resurrection stories as there are women and men who are empowered by God's grace to keep on keeping on.

There are as many resurrection stories as there are women and men who greet the new day because the love let loose today is born to us by another, by someone who finds us standing alone, weeping by the tombs and captivities of our life, and who calls us by name.

By that gesture we are nourished by nothing less than life eternal, and sent out to tell an unbelieving, anxious, and worried world, "We have seen the Lord."

"Christ is risen. He is risen indeed!"

This is all that matters!

11. EASTERTIDE
JOHN 10:1–10
"MORE LIFE THAN BEFORE"

1

Important differences distinguish Jews, Muslims, and Christians from one another. But one feature that they share is the special regard each has for a book.

Faithful Muslims revere the Q'uran, because they believe that in it the Prophet Mohammed has faithfully transmitted the true teaching of the One who is God, Allah the All-Compassionate One.

Faithful religious Jews revere the Hebrew Scriptures, texts that early Christians reshaped into the Old Testament, because they believe in that book God has revealed the laws and the precepts that should guide and direct the life of the people delivered from bondage.

Although faithful Christians esteem the Old Testament, we especially revere the New Testament, but for very different reasons.

Teachings there are here aplenty. Precepts and moral advice abound. But we attend to the New Testament, and especially to the four Gospels with which it begins. But we do not do so primarily for the teachings and moral guidance that they contain. But for the story of a really lived life that they present.

For it is here in the Gospels that we have access to the *life* of Jesus, not just to his teachings and moral counsel, so valuable as his teachings and counsel are. And for this we can be truly grateful.

Because the Christian way of life is not just learning Jesus' teachings and taking them to heart—which we are, of course to do. But the Christian way of life is trying to conform our lives to his. For in Christ, God seeks to mend all the wounded women and men of the world. In Christ the divine care has come to embrace the life of the whole of humankind.

So it is very important that each of the New Testament Gospel writers has written a Jesus story, not just organized a collection of Jesus words. For the life of faith is better served by attending to his life—to what he *did* as well as to what he *said,* and more importantly, to *who* he was.

2

Jesus of Nazareth was a teacher of rare moral insight. He helped others to see that God's request touches our heart as well as our hands. And he insisted that God looks on our motives as well as our actions. And for this we are grateful. But the basic Christian claim is not about the teachings of Jesus.

Jesus of Nazareth was a first-century Palestinian Jew who lived his life in obedience to God and gave his life in service to others. And for that we are grateful. But the basic Christian claim is not about his surprising and upsetting deeds.

The basic Christian claim is, rather, that in the whole course of Jesus' life the power and compassion of God have entered the world in a new and clearer way.

In the life of Christ everything we believed about power has been changed. Jesus has power, but it is no longer power to overwhelm, but power to nurture and enhance our best efforts to love the good things and beings of God's world in a grateful, non-grasping way.

In the life of Christ everything we believed about compassion has been changed. Jesus pours out upon us great compassion, but it is no longer compassion to heal our hurts alone, but compassion to overcome our inattention to others—the forgotten, the marginal, the ignored, the neglected.

Jesus is the man in whom the divine presence has taken up permanent residence where all women and men live.

3

In the Gospel appointed for today [John 10:1–10], St. John adds more images to the portrait he has been drawing of this Jesus, who embodies the power and compassion of God in such a new and saving way.

He will shortly speak of Jesus as the "true vine," who gives life to all the branches joined to him. And he has already characterized him as the "living water' and the "bread of life" who sustains all who journey with him.

And now he speaks of Jesus as the "good shepherd" who calls his sheep by name. And he speaks of Jesus as the "gate of the sheepfold," the doorway into the green pastures of which the psalmist sang. [Psalm 23]

"True vine," "living water," "bread of life," "good shepherd," "gate of the sheepfold"—St. John uses all of these pictures to illuminate, to clarify, to illustrate the bold declaration with which the Gospel began: "and the Word became flesh and lived among us. . . . from his fullness we have all received, grace upon grace."

Because of this divine condescension, Jesus can now make the promise with which today's reading ends: "I came that they may have life, and have it abundantly." Another translator has put it this way: Jesus said, "I came that they may have far more life than before, have it to the full."

The life of the redeemed people of God is not really a matter of quantity, as if one could have more or less of it. It is a different kind of life altogether—full of hope, forgiveness, second chances; full of joy, reconciliation and eternal peace.

With the promise of "abundant life," of "far more life than before," we, who need all the help we can get, have been given the help we most deeply need:

- not another reminder of what we should be doing. We already know that the divine demand sends us to do whatever love needs to have done.
- not more answers to our troubling questions, as if a new explanation were going to reduce the mystery of living in the time God has provided for us.
- not another teaching, as if any words could diminish our amazement that God should care for us.

"I came that they may have far more life than before, have it to the full." In this promise, we have been given a bequest of hope, and the courage to live out the divine generosity without attempting to prove ourselves ever again.

With his promise, we have been given the company of God's own self—to heal, to nudge, to give solace, and always to overshadow us.

This is the abundant life that awaits us at every Eucharist.

This is the life, "far more life than before," that we receive so thankfully whenever we break bread together.

Nourished by the abundance of the life he bestows on us, we can give praise to God, whose mercy surrounds us, whose forgiveness makes new beginnings for us, and whose grace empowers us to be for one another.

12. EASTERTIDE
JOHN 14:1–6
"LET NOT YOUR HEART BE TROUBLED"

1

This is the fifth Sunday *of* Easter. But there may be some of you who can recall that the older Prayer Book named this the Fifth Sunday *after* Easter.

Now the change from calling these Sundays *after* to Sundays *of* Easter may seem to be a very small thing indeed. But how we name these days is really more significant than it might seem at first.

Each Sunday in the church year has its own name or number. These markers are signposts that help us negotiate our way from Advent and Epiphany, through Lent, to Easter and Pentecost, and finally to Advent again.

This is our annual rehearsal of the life of Christ. It is so arranged that we may be encouraged to conform our lives more deeply to his: the expectancy of Advent, the sobriety of Lent, the jubilation of Easter. But this means we need to note where we are each week if our faith is to benefit most fully from the liturgical calendar.

These Sundays following Easter Day are now properly designated Sundays *of* Easter, not Sundays *after* Easter. For we are now in Eastertide, the great fifty days between Easter Day and the Feast of Pentecost.

To say of these days that they are Sundays *after* Easter might suggest that Easter is over and done with. But Easter is the permanent presence of hope.

To say of these days that they are Sundays *after* Easter might suggest that Easter is over and done with. But Easter is the continuing empowerment of grace.

To say of these days that they are Sundays *after* Easter might suggest that Easter is over and done with. But Easter is the great "nevertheless" of amazement that faith shouts against everything that makes for death and hatred.

Easter is the great "nevertheless" of wonder that faith shouts against everything that makes for cruelty and despair. Easter is the great "nevertheless" that raises us up out of indolence and joylessness.

The lighted Paschal Candle that burns these fifty days from Easter Day to Pentecost is the sign of this grateful and awesome "nevertheless."

This flame reminds us that we have been born again to hope. This flame reminds us that we who are faced with a world of pain and suffering really can survive by the great love that is stronger than death.

2

We are reminded as well of the quality of this life that Easter Day inaugurates by the readings appointed for these Sundays *of* Easter.

First, as Eastertide began, we heard how the risen Christ enheartens his disciples as he makes himself known to them in the breaking of the bread. And on every Sunday since that first Eucharist at Emmaus, the risen Christ has been present to his people in the bread broken and the wine poured out for the remembrance of him.

Then, we heard how the risen Christ gives his peace, his most precious gift, to this disciples shut up in their room in fear. And on every Sunday since his appearance to Thomas, that great peace has been shared in the colonies of the faithful. The peace we share is not just neighborly camaraderie, but the comforting presence of the risen Christ himself.

Last week, we heard of Christ the Good Shepherd, who calls each of his sheep by name, and who gives abundant life, more life than ever before.

Next week, we will hear of Christ the True Vine, who nourishes all whose lives are linked with his, and so bids us and enables us to bear fruit. Bearing the fruit of believing is to do justice, to be there for others, and to do those acts of care that make Christ present to a grieving and fractured world.

3

And today, on this Fifth Sunday *of* Easter, we have just heard Jesus' counsel to us that no matter how sad, no matter how perplexing, no matter how worrisome the day may be, we are not to let our hearts be troubled.

Not because the sadness and the perplexity and the worry will disappear, but because, as he said, "In my Father's house are many mansions."

And the entrance to that heavenly house is not hidden or obscure, or hard to find. or, as he said, "I am the way, the truth, and the life."

Perhaps you noticed that I used the term "many mansions" from the King James Version of 1611. Most contemporary translations have dropped "mansions," and refer instead to "many rooms" or "dwelling places." No translation from one language to another can ever give a perfect rendering of the original. But "mansions" has always seemed to me to convey the suggestion that there is really lots and lots of space in our Father's house, more pointedly than simply "many rooms."

Jesus' reminder that "in my Father's house there are many mansions," and his comforting injunction that we should not let our "hearts be troubled," is the Gospel text regularly heard in the burial office. And so these words have become a central part of our Christian consciousness.

But at moments of sorrow and sadness, that these words seek to assuage, we are not always able to hear them clearly.

For we may be remembering the one we have lost, or are too grieved to think of much of anything. Then we may hear Jesus' words of solace, but not really hear them. For we may be wondering what our life will be like without the relationships that had nourished and sustained us for so long or for so short a time.

And that is alright. When Jesus says, "Let not your heart be troubled," he makes it alright to grieve and to be sorrowful. His promise lets sorrow have its time and place. And then helps us get up and be about the necessary work of our world.

We need to hear his promise, not so much and always at the time of death. We need to hear his promise now and anytime, seeing that we know not what a day may bring forth.

For in the light of his promise we are bidden to move from each day to the next, knowing that confidence and hope are not vain delusions, but the deepest truth about the life we have been given by God.

Our presence before God does not depend on who we are, or where we have been; nor on what we have achieved, or on what we have failed in. Our presence before God is based on the secure knowledge that we are loved—in life, and in death, and in life beyond death.

We do not have to succeed, only to remain faithful.

13. ASCENSION DAY
ACTS 1:1–11
"WHY DO YOU STAND LOOKING UP TOWARD HEAVEN?"

1

The Collect and the first reading for this Seventh Sunday *of* Easter remind us that this is also the Sunday after Ascension Day.

The story of Ascension Day that St. Luke tells in *the Acts of the Apostles* conveys a very important Christian insight. But it is not easy for our modern ears to hear this story and to make any sense of it. For on all counts, this is a very strange tale: the Risen Christ appears to his followers, and then, while he is speaking with them, he disappears.

The narrative St. Luke provides is a spare one indeed. The author says of Jesus simply that he was "lifted up," and that he vanished from sight. Subsequent centuries of Christian art have pictured this event by showing Jesus rising up into the sky on a cloud.

Now every school child that has opened a science book in the last hundred years, or who has heard or seen anything about space flight, knows for sure that there is something very strange in this story.

We all know that the universe is simply not the way that St. Luke and everybody else in the first century thought it was.

We all know that there is no "up," no place up there to go in space, even when one escapes the earth's gravitational pull.

We all know that "heaven" is not a place up there that one could reach by riding clouds, or by some other means of celestial transportation.

And St. Luke's story is not the only source of our difficulty. The Jesus of St. John's Gospel reminds or reassures his friends and us by saying "I go to the Father." And the ancient creeds of the Church say of the risen Christ that "he ascended into heaven, and sits at the right hand of God the Father."

2

Now there is no virtue in trying to believe on Sunday what we know to be false the rest of the week. So what are we to do with this strange story? What can we make of this fanciful tale and still hold on to our faith?

We could simply *discard* it. And thus remove all the Ascension language from our liturgy, and delete Ascension Day from the Church's calendar.

We could *ignore* it. And pretend that it is not there, or read over the service so quickly, or so diffidently, that people might not notice it.

We could *rewrite* it. So that it would conform to the modern scientific understanding of the universe.

But as tempting as these alternatives might appear, they all seem inappropriate, and headed in the wrong direction.

As tempting as these options might appear, they all ask us to sever our continuity with the early generations of Christian experience. And that would be an unacceptable loss.

But these options are misguided for another and more significant reason. As tempting as these ways of dealing with the oddness of the Ascension story might be, they all ask us to pretend that the language of faith is only the prosaic language of history, with no room for the poetic language of the imagination.

The Church's language about "heaven" and "ascension" is simply picture language. It is an attempt to talk in images about some of the deepest realities of Christian faith that are difficult to express in any other way.

The Church's language about "heaven" is simply an attempt to draw a picture of our hope of life with God, an image of our continuing life in God's presence.

There does not seem to be any ordinary way to say that. And so we resort to drawing word pictures.

The true meaning of the Ascension story does not depend on the false, prescientific view of the universe it presupposes.

The true meaning of the doctrine of the Ascension does not depend on the image of Jesus as a space traveler, or as a master of the art of levitation.

St. Luke himself suggests this indirectly in his account in the Book of *Acts*. The message Jesus' followers hear is "Why do you stand looking up toward heaven?"

"Get on with your mission for Christ in the world. There is no point in speculating, in trying to guess how it happened, or even about what happened. The only point is to be up and doing what the Lord invites and enables us to do."

3

The Ascension story or doctrine says very little that is new or different from what Easter Day proclaims: This Jesus of Nazareth, this earthly-historical Jesus, this Palestinian Jewish teacher; this friend of women, the outcast and the disinherited; this Son of Mary who accepts all those that everybody else thinks are unacceptable; this Jesus has ascended.

That means, this Jesus is set free from Palestine, set free from all particular geographical places, to be present with us in all places.

That means, this Jesus is set free from the first century, free from all particular times, to be present with us in all times.

He has ascended; that is, he is set free to be the Christ for everyone in all places and at all times. This Jesus is God's gift to the whole world.

So, "Why do you stand looking up toward heaven?"

He in whom God has come to be our closest neighbor, empowers us to become a neighbor in his name to all the sad, the hurt, and the dispossessed.

He in whom God has come to be our closest neighbor, empowers us to become a neighbor to all the hungry, the lonely, and the guilty.

We have work to do in his name. And his Spirit in our midst turns us away from "looking up toward heaven." Instead he asks us to look out all around us. There is some caring work for us to do there.

14. PENTECOST
I CORINTHIANS 12:7
"THE LORD, THE GIVER OF LIFE"

1

The great fifty days of Eastertide began, and now end, with a surprise. This unexpected turn-of-events shatters the world, and divides time for ever. At the beginning of Eastertide, the newly risen Jesus appears. At the ending, the newly born Church appears. Both raised from the dead and given new life.

"Christ is Risen," we proclaimed on Easter Day. And on this day of Pentecost, we could say "The Church is Risen." For today we celebrate the Holy Spirit's raising up the Church, and giving new life to this company of forgiven and forgiving sinners and justice-makers.

Jesus' friends and enemies alike thought that his life had been ended by the crucifixion. But now it was transformed and exalted. The little group of his broken-hearted and dispirited disciples had given up, but now were themselves given new life and new purpose.

Before two decades will have passed, St. Paul will say to the little Christian colony in Corinth, "If anyone is in Christ, there is a new creation; everything old has passed away. See, everything old has passed away." [II Cor 5:17]

And three centuries later, the creed we soon will say together will sum up this conviction by acknowledging the Church's belief in "the Holy Spirit, the Lord, the Giver of Life."

The Feast of Pentecost is the annual reminder that the Church is inaugurated by the Spirit, is filled with the Spirit, is authorized by the Spirit, and empowered by the Spirit to be Christ's company of conscience and compassion to a wounded and fallen world.

2

But there are many spirits abroad in the land these days and in the churches as well. And it is not always easy to tell which of these spirits and voices express the divine will, and which are demonic appeals masquerading as the divine. How can we know if the voices and spirits we hear invite us to life rather than to death? How can we tell if the voices and spirits we hear are divine or demonic?

St. Paul answered that question in his letters to the Corinthian Christians: "To each is given the manifestation of the Spirit *for the common good.* [I Cor 12:7]

So if the spirit that calls, moves us to build up the community of faith, with no need for private gain, it may be the Holy Spirit of God.

If the spirit that calls, leads us to thoughtful speech, and to shun unthinking ecstasy, it may be the Holy Spirit of God.

If the spirit that calls, pushes us into serious service of the neglected and powerless, and frees us from thinking that we need an exciting, emotional high, it may be the Holy Spirit of God.

If the spirit that calls, helps us to be agents of good, and not to worry about feeling good, it may be the Holy Spirit of God.

If the spirit that calls, turns us to the other with care and compassion, and away from self-worry, it may be the Holy Spirit of God.

If the spirit that calls, helps us to cherish difference, and to avoid a craving for religious certitude, it may be the Holy Spirit of God.

If the spirit that calls, lures us to love the unloved, and to give up waiting to be deeply moved, it may be the Holy Spirit of God.

If the spirit that calls, moves us to praise and not condemn, and moves us to seek justice for all, instead of advantage for some, it may be the Holy Spirit of God.

3

But the Spirit who empowers and keeps company with us is not given over to us as our possession. The presence of the Holy Spirit of God in our midst is the sign of our being possessed by God, and made God's people, not our own.

St. Paul announces that "All who are led by the Spirit of God are children of God." [Rom 8:14] And in his letters he reminds us again and again that being led by the Spirit of God means that we are all gifted persons. Every one of us, by virtue of our baptism, is a gifted person.

This means—that there is no room for boasting that we have made it on our own.

This means—that there is no ground for exalting ourselves over anyone else.

This means—that there is no basis for thinking that we have nothing to contribute to the wellbeing and mission of the Church.

For all that we are and all that we have we have received as a gift from another. In the community of faith, the spirit of any one person dominating another has been put aside forever. In the community of faith, the plea of any persons to say that they cannot help has been set aside for ever.

We rejoice always whenever a bishop confers Holy Orders. For this is the gift of the Holy Spirit on which the very life of the Church depends.

But there are other gifts on which the Church depends as well, and many of these are not quite so important-sounding as: priesthood, diaconate, preaching, teaching.

Sometimes the gifts of the Spirit on which the Church relies on are given quietly, with no fanfare, with no promise of perfection, only the promise of help.

Sometimes the gifts of the Spirit that the Church relies on may seem to have little theological history or doctrinal status, but they have mighty importance for the upbuilding of the common good:

- the gift of listening, the gift of smiling;
- the gift of patience, the gift of waiting;
- the gift of asking, the gift of presence;
-• the gift of stepping aside;
- the gift of just being there, the ministry of presence.

The Body of Christ needs them all. They are gifts of the Holy Spirit, the "Lord and Giver of Life," as surely as the call to the sacramental priesthood and the teaching ministry. They are some of the gifts of the Spirit that make a company of women and men, with all our mistakes and imperfections, sometimes to be the Church Christ intends, and to be the Church that the world needs.

NOTES

1. Source reference is lost.
2. Reference is lost.
3. Bill Moyers' interview with the Rev. William Sloane Coffin, March 5, 2004.
4. Paul Rudnick, *Jeffrey* [1994].

Chapter Six

Living an Epiphany

1

I turn first to a different story—my own—before attending to St. Matthew's narrative [Mth 2:1–12 KJV] of the improbable but salvific birth that we respect this night.

Some of you know parts or all of this story. I came to Colgate University in 1957 as chaplain and a member of the teaching faculty. I had been ordained some years earlier in one of the Protestant bodies now part of the United Church of Christ. After several years, I moved out of the chaplaincy and into full-time teaching. This move left my Sundays free. And I was able then to act on my long-standing interest in the Episcopal Church.

This was an attraction that had begun when I sang in the choir for the Christmas Eve Midnight Mass in the heavily censed Anglo-Catholic sanctuary of St. James' Episcopal Church on South Sixth Street, in Goshen, Indiana. On that December night 67 years ago I was encompassed and possessed by an epiphany of truth and permission whose grace has enlivened and guarded my soul ever since.

The Hamilton part of this journey began in Lent 1964. The Lenten observance at St. Thomas' Church in those days, as in most parishes, offered a Wednesday evening celebration of the Holy Eucharist, always called then "the Holy Communion." I began to attend these services from Ash Wednesday on and received the sacrament each week. I was also quite aware of the rubric in the 1928 Prayer Book that governed such things: "There shall none be admitted to the Holy Communion, until such time as he be confirmed, or ready and desirous to be confirmed." [1928 PB, p. 299]

And so I was not surprised to be invited for coffee by the rector, the Rev. H. Harrison Hadley, after the last of the Wednesday services. [We seldom used here the title "Father" back then.] The conversation that evening set in motion the steps that led in 1965 to Wanda's and my confirmation by Bishop Higley.

This was done at a specially arranged mid-week afternoon service, attended by most of the little Anglican colony on Colgate's faculty and staff. [Their situation had progressed by then from the 1890's, when a faculty member is said to have been publicly reprimanded at the monthly Faculty Meeting for having attended a service "according to the Book of Common Prayer."]

I remember here those who were at that Confirmation service, and who are now in that small but great cloud of witnesses, whose "glorias" and "alleluias" surround us this night, cheering us on:[1] I think especially of Molly and Warren Ramshaw [Warren was the parish's first License Lay Reader, and his coming to Hamilton worried the Rector a bit about just what he might be permitted to do, for we had not had a Lay Reader before]. Molly sometimes read the Lessons, and always with the rehearsed care of a professional actor. I can see the Organist and Choirmaster Bob Murray and Marj. [We sometimes had choir rehearsals at their house, where he could use his own personal pipe organ.] I see Perry Rockafellow, the tennis coach, and his wife Dorothy, with whom I sang in Gilbert and Sullivan's *The Gondoliers*, my first spring in Hamilton. [The addition of the choir room is named in honor of their young son Wade, who had died in a tragic accident.] I remember as well the psychologist and Student Advisor George Estabrooks. And there was David Trainer. [His family electrified the bell ringing after his death, so fitting, as he was always the one who pulled the old bell ropes before the services.]

I remember especially the distinguished and gracious Gertrude Edgarton, the president's secretary, as such indispensable persons were called then. I learned from her to reverence the Cross as it passes by in the procession, and to appreciate the old Eucharistic hymn of St. Thomas' Aquinas, "O Saving Victim, Opening Wide the Gate of Heaven to Us Below." [*Hymnal 1982,* No. 310]

I eventually sat for the diocesan ordination examinations in the last year before these tests became general and uniform throughout the whole Church. The central essay question was to discuss the theology of the Prayer of Humble Access: "We do not come to this thy table, O Lord, trusting in our own righteousness, but in thy manifold and great mercies." [Priests back then were just beginning to invite the congregation to join in that prayer, although the rubric quite explicitly said "Then shall the Priest, kneeling down at the Lord's Table, say, in the name of all those who shall receive the Communion, this Prayer following."]

Bishop Higley admitted that he did not quite know what to do with me, so he turned me over to his Coadjutor—Ned Cole—who fine-tuned my Anglican sensibility as best as he could for one whose sympathies hovered between Low and Broad churchmanship. I was eventually [1972] ordained to the Sacred Order of Priests by Bishop Cole in this very room, and before this very altar.

I began, then, on weekends, to supply various parishes throughout the diocese, while, at the same time, continuing to meet my faculty responsibilities. Over the years I have preached and presided at the altars of more than forty parishes in the diocese, some for quite extended periods: Fourteen years at St. George's Church in Chadwicks. But shorter periods at Earlville, Sherburne, Chenango Bridge, Mexico, New Hartford, Utica, Camden, Clinton, Baldwinsville, Sherrill, DeWitt, and Chittenango, among others, with long stops at St. Thomas' Church in Hamilton. Someone said that at one time I probably knew more people in more parishes than anyone in the diocese, other than the bishop. And so attending Diocesan Convention was something like going to a great reunion of names and faces and memories. I miss that.

And now I have come full circle, ending the public exercise of my priesthood right here where it was first authorized by the Laying on of Hands by our bishop, with the apostolic authority he has, in succession from the Church's beginning, and, as we believe, with Christ's own intention.

I will continue to write, and even preach when invited to do so, but I do not anticipate presiding again at the altar, what the older Prayer Book called "the Holy Table," or sometimes "the Lord's Table." Decreasing mobility and problems of balance have made my continuing to do that more and more imprudent. My doctor's name for this is "degenerative lumbar spinal stenosis." That means: my back hurts; it is difficult for me to stand straight unaided for long; and I find it hard to walk very far without my cane.

2

But our chief concern tonight is not the turns of this personal story with which I have begun, but St. Matthew's special way of telling the most important story that has ever been told. This is the story of a risky, unattended birth to a not-quite-married Jewish teenager, in the little Palestinian town of Bethlehem, then under oppressive enemy occupation, just as it still is today.

Unlike St. Luke's account, in this Gospel there is no smelly stable, no manger, no "sore afraid" shepherds, no angelic chorus announcing "Peace on earth." Here Joseph and Mary are living in Bethlehem, and Jesus is born in their house. Some travelling astrologers have found their starry way there.

They not only present some extraordinary gifts, but, as Matthew says, they "fell down and worshipped him." They thus became the first, and foreigners at that, to recognize the divinity of the career begun this night.

Matthew and Luke agree that God did not work out the hope for our rescue and rehabilitation by some dramatic gesture, by a great public demonstration of power. They both know that God did all of this simply by a birth. But of course a birth is not all that simple, then or now. God did this with all the hope and danger that attend every birth, but especially one with no physician, or no midwife present to help. Every mother here and hopefully every father as well, know just how fragile, how chancy, how much at risk a new-born baby and his mother are, in even the best of situations.

St. Matthew knows nothing about a stable and straw, a manger, the darkness and the cow dung. But attend to the police patrols and the suspicious neighbors. And remember what St. Matthew does know—a Bethlehem house, a likely most modest space, with the winter's cold, an eerily moving star, and some alien visitors bearing such remarkable gifts that they portend the sometime death of this divinely royal child.

This is the Gospel story of our redemption, begun this night with the accord and agency of the Blessed Mother Mary; begun this night by glorious agents of the whole non-Jewish world. For this little Jewish boy will one day open the windows of God's blessing for all humankind.

In the birth of this child God has invested our ordinary and transitory life, with all its risks and misadventures and accidents, with surprising pleasure, and has flooded this very ordinary and transitory life with extraordinary and unending showers of grace.

3

The upbuilding gift of grace born anew this night and witnessed by wise men from the East is the promise of God's saving presence that helps us to live patiently with all those things that cannot be changed, to live with our limitations and our infirmities with acceptance and without struggle or defiance.

God benevolence displayed this Epiphany night has erased the marks of our sin. But dealing with the quite natural movement from our birth to our death is another matter altogether. The Gospel is the good news that our confession has been heard, and that our mistakes, our missteps and our moral failures have been deleted from the hard disk of our lives.

But our bad backs have not been cured, even by the blessings of this season. Yet we can still rejoice, for the Gospel that Christmas announces and that Epiphany enlarges, assures us that God has come to be with us right here where we are—with our aches and hazards, with our discomfort and imbalance. Just as God came to be with that young girl from Nazareth in her unplanned pregnancy—the Blessed Mother Mary. This was a most unexpected event, but one that would come to change the world and save us all.

This birth now revealed to the whole world is the sure promise that no matter where we have been, no matter what we have done, that whatever shape we are in, no matter how tired or tired of we may be, that no matter how crippled or worn out we may be or may feel, the One born this night and shown to the world has come to hold our arm as we walk into our next day, wherever that may lead us.

NOTE

1. Several other Episcopal faculty and staff were not able to be present at the Confirmation Service: Alfred Seely Brown [chemistry], Mark Randall [swimming coach], Howard Pike [purchasing agent].

Other Books by Donald L. Berry

Mutuality: The Vision of Martin Buber [Albany, State University of New York Press, 1985]
Travelers Advisory [Lewiston: The Edwin Mellen Press, 1990] [Mellen Poetry Series volume 9]
An Inquiry into the Nature and Usefulness of a Perspectival Approach to the Study of Religion [Lewiston: The Edwin Mellen Press, 1991]
Through a Glass Darkly: The Ambiguity of the Christian Tradition [Lanham, Md., University Press of America, 2006]
Holy Words and Holy Orders: As Dying, Behold We Live [Lanham, Md., University Press of America, 2009]

Breinigsville, PA USA
23 November 2010
249879BV00002B/5/P